D1526249

BLACK
MARKET
MONEY

THE COLLAPSE
OF U.S. MILITARY
CURRENCY CONTROL
IN WORLD WAR II

BLACK
MARKET
MONEY

Walter Rundell, Jr.

LOUISIANA STATE UNIVERSITY PRESS : 1964

B+T
3.40
10-2-64
11-9-64

FOR MY PARENTS

Walter Rundell
and
Olive Spillar Rundell

. . . money was the sinews of war . . .

Preface | BLACK-MARKET MONEY

THE relationship between money and war has many facets. Modern warfare distinctly demands inordinate expenditures which are supported by taxation of citizens, by deficit financing, and in the case of victor nations, by levies on the defeated. The scope of this phase of wartime finance is immense—and largely beyond the boundaries of this study. A more personal interaction of money and war concerns the problem of currency in the hands of soldiers and the efforts of military authorities to exert some control over the currency. My objective is to describe and analyze the American military experience with currency control in World War II. Currency control, for these purposes, can best be defined as the Army's regulation of conversions of foreign currencies for servicemen so that no greater sums in foreign currencies were exchanged for dollars than had been disbursed as pay and allowances.

Army records were the primary source of material; additional pertinent documents from other governmental agencies have also been used. Although the Army's experience in the realm of currency control was easily the most extensive of all the armed forces, the other services undoubtedly had some encounter with the problem. Since I have not investigated their records, I make no claim that this study is a comprehensive treatment of the currency control challenges presented to all American fighting forces. In World War II the Air Corps was still an organic part of the Army, therefore the research covered Air Corps activities.

Notwithstanding the fact that the volume's title specifies the period as World War II, the study extends beyond the end of hostilities through the first year of occupation because the problems of currency control created by the war did not cease with the end of hostilities, but spun themselves out fully in the initial year of occupation. The post-hostilities situation so obviously had its seeds in wartime policy that it would be a misrepresentation to pretend that the story concluded on V-J Day.

My basic assumption in approaching the problem of currency control is that the government owed members of the Army no money beyond the pay and allowances specified for their rank, type of duty, and length of service. Soldiers were fully entitled to all legal pay and allowances, including dependency benefits, but no more. (The term "soldiers" includes all members of the Army. This usage is less cumbersome than the technical distinction sometimes made between soldiers [enlisted men] and officers.) From the standpoint of the government's stake in currency control, it would not have mattered how much pay Congress had appropriated for the Army, as long as soldiers were limited to receiving their just remunerations. The argument, then, is not against adequate compensation for soldiers, but against soldiers contravening exchange regulations in such a way as to receive more money than they were entitled to.

Arguments have been forwarded that currency control violations really hurt no one; that soldiers who had been through the heat of battle deserved an excursion into illicit finance; and that if the government lost money, soldiers, as American citizens, gained. The obvious fallacy in this point of view is that the rewards of currency control violations went to those willing to break laws and disobey Army orders. The soldier who refrained from involvement in illicit fiscal negotiations would actually be discriminated against economically for comporting himself according to the letter of the law. Surely it would not be consonant with traditional American ideals to condone illegal methods to secure public monies, nor would it be in harmony with the Army's concept of discipline to reward furtively those who disregarded Army policy.

Some military officials had argued for a currency control policy predicated upon the fact that the Army was composed largely of citizen-soldiers. Whether the policy-makers who decided to subvert currency control because of this situation correctly judged the attitudes of the citizen-soldiers and the country at large cannot be determined. Perhaps a good bit less deference could have been paid to the attitudes of these civilians in uniform, as far as currency control procedures were concerned. On the other hand, the policy-makers might have judged precisely the temper of citizen-soldiers and the nation behind them, and thereby provided essential loopholes. The decisions might have been the result of shrewd psychological insight, or they might have allowed an undue latitude that promoted a lack of both military- and self-discipline and a loosening of the moral fiber of servicemen. Right or wrong, many currency control policies proceeded from assumptions that the Army could not maintain the type of discipline over citizen-soldiers that might be expected of career militarists. Since the Army usually paid lip service to maintaining currency control however, there is an indication that lapses were more the result of mismanagement than intentional policy. But at the same time, some of the greatest lapses resulted from decisions based largely on the desire to placate citizen-soldiers.

The Army clearly needed to maintain a high morale to infuse soldiers with every possible incentive to fight toward victory. But to state that the Army provided the opportunity for circumventing its own currency control program to strengthen morale is to assume it willfully encouraged dishonesty. Certainly this was no way to instill a uniformly high level of morale! Indeed, in the occupation period all indications were that the slipshod currency control program, which allowed personal deviousness, proved to be a major factor in low morale throughout the European theater. If the Army intended to maintain respect for itself in the eyes of both its members and occupied nations—and this is the only conceivable intent —it could not have afforded to project a public image of being serious about achieving currency control while it was tacitly encouraging violations. Therefore, any intentional policy of this nature should be discounted.

When the Army exchanged more foreign currency than it had disbursed as pay and allowances, the government lost money. There were many ways to camouflage such losses and make them appear less consequential than they were, but the fact remains that these losses were eventually and ultimately transferred to American tax-payers. With the immense vogue for deficit financing by the government and the comforting argument that the government's unbalanced budget reflects a healthy economy, the loss through currency control violations of merely half a billion dollars plus might cause scant alarm. Somewhere, however, directly or indirectly, the loss had to be recouped from the taxes paid by citizens. Consequently, the government's loss was finally that of its citizens.

In the ensuing study of currency control in World War II, one overriding factor must be borne in mind: currency control was merely a subsidiary function of prosecuting the war. The major consideration for the Army (as an instrument of national policy) in any strategic or tactical planning was the fight for victory, not the maintenance of currency control. If the battle of currency control was lost, it was a comparatively minor skirmish, largely an unhappy aftermath of the fighting. Certainly it was a skirmish worth studying, for it had broad implications.

Although this volume concerns a military topic, I have tried to deal with military terminology in such a way that the general reader will have no difficulty. When discussing overseas commands, I have used short titles rather than the official designations, e.g., European theater rather than European Theater of Operations, United States Army, perhaps sacrificing a small degree of precision for clarity and readability. Likewise, I have refrained from employing military abbreviations and symbols wherever possible. In some cases, however, the symbol remains the only practical device. Instead of using assistant chief of staff for personnel, it is much simpler to use G-1 (especially since there is no satisfactory short form). When I use the staff positions, G-1 through G-5 (with initial identifications), I subsequently will refer to them in the third person singular, since the designation ultimately applied to an individual staff member within a large staff section.

Research in the primary sources for this volume was done in the General Services Administration's Federal Records Center, Kansas City, Missouri, and the World War II Records Division, Office of

Military Records, National Archives and Records Service. I wish to extend my genuine appreciation to the staffs of these two depositories for their uniformly efficient and friendly service. Moreover, I acknowledge the great assistance of the staff of the Library of Congress. Both the Office of the Chief of Finance and the Office of the Chief of Military History, Department of the Army, made their extensive files available to me and furnished valuable counsel. Without the aid of both offices, this study would have been impossible.

In the course of my work, I incurred many scholarly debts. While it would be impossible to acknowledge the assistance I have received from all who contributed something to my project, I would like to offer a special word of thanks to Professor Edith H. Parker of Del Mar College, who first directed my attention toward this subject; Dr. Ernst Posner, former chairman of the Department of History and dean of the Graduate School of the American University; Professors Louis C. Hunter and Arthur A. Ekirch, Jr., of the American University; Dr. Stanley L. Falk of the Industrial College of the Armed Forces; Lieutenant Colonel George Shepard of the Office of the Chief of Finance; Dr. Boyd C. Shafer, former Executive Secretary of the American Historical Association; and Professor John Duffy of the University of Pittsburgh.

Professor John W. Caughey, editor of the *Pacific Historical Review,* has generously granted permission to reprint in a somewhat expanded form material that was originally published in that journal.

I want to pay the traditional, but nonetheless sincere, tribute to the uxorial virtues that contributed to the publication of this volume. My wife, Deanna Boyd Rundell, has been a constant source of enthusiasm and support. Shelley has helped, too, in her way.

WALTER RUNDELL, JR.

Contents | BLACK-MARKET MONEY

PREFACE   vii

Chapter 1 The Objectives   3

2 Wartime Practices: Foundation for Failure   13

3 Wartime Policy-Making for Europe   31

4 Europe: The Debacle   41

5 The Far East   61

6 Currency Control Books   69

7 Success with Scrip   80

NOTES   93
BIBLIOGRAPHY   111
INDEX   117

BLACK
MARKET
MONEY

| *Chapter 1* | # The Objectives |

THE United States Army's problem of currency control in World War II was basically a matter of regulating the amount of foreign money soldiers could exchange for American dollars. The desired goal was to exchange no more foreign money into dollars than soldiers had received as pay. American troops overseas were normally paid in indigenous currencies because most Allied nations demanded their use, fearing that a wholesale usage of dollars would disrupt their economies.[1] American soldiers, although paid in alien currencies, were entitled to exchange their pay into dollars since it was prescribed in dollars by Congressional legislation.

While overseas, soldiers were not actually permitted to exchange their pay for dollars, but they were allowed to exchange it for "dollar credits." These dollar credits resulted from transfers of pay to the United States through such means as postal money orders or the personal transfer account. A man could also establish dollar credits by putting pay into war bonds and soldier's deposits.[2] When the Army established dollar credits for its men, it always used the official rate of exchange between the foreign currency in which the men were paid and the dollar so that the troops incurred no loss.

Had American soldiers been content to offer for exchange only money they had received from the pay table, there would have been no currency control problem, for the Army would have been exchanging only the money that it had disbursed as pay and allowances. But when it began to exchange more money for soldiers than it had paid them, currency control broke down. *Here* was the fundamental problem; for the Army, in making these exchanges, was actually drawing on funds for which no Congressional appropriation existed. The money which soldiers offered for exchange in excess of their pay invariably came from the black market or other unofficial channels.

The initial difficulty the Army faced in the realm of currency control was that it realized too late the immensity of the problem it confronted. The problem had developed to monumental proportions before the War Department began to consider remedial action. Then the War Department's action was misguided in that it never tried to enforce ironclad restrictions on the amount of pay a soldier could exchange. The only way the Army could have achieved control, still paying with indigenous currency, was to have specified that no soldier could exchange more money than he had drawn across the pay table. Such a simple but effective restriction was never imposed. Instead, the Army relied on a series of inconsistent and inadequate currency control policies.

One reason the Army was unprepared to cope with wartime currency control was that prewar planning had been insufficient. The Office of the Chief of Finance, which was charged with disbursing and accounting for funds Congress appropriated for the Army, was the most logical branch of the Army to plan a currency control program. But a brief excursion into the background of the Office of the Chief of Finance and its Army-wide functional division, the finance department, might give some indication of the inadequacy of planning for currency control.

At the head of the finance department was the chief of finance, a major general. Immediately prior to and during World War II, the chief of finance was Major General Howard K. Loughry. Perhaps the total picture of military finances would have been brighter if his interest in currency control, as well as in other vital fiscal activities of the Army, had been keener. Since General Loughry had not geared his department's activities to meet the enormous challenges of the war, he was not appointed fiscal director when the

Army Service Forces organized the Office of the Fiscal Director in 1942 as the Army's highest-level finance agency. His record spoke against him.[3] A civilian who was a senior partner in the accounting firm of Haskins and Sells, Arthur H. Carter, was chosen for the post and appointed as a major general.

With the chief of finance removed from the key policy-making position, the Office of the Chief of Finance was no longer in so favorable a position to formulate fiscal policy as it would have occupied if its chief had exercised the power that should normally have been his. Consequently, fiscal policy-making devolved by default to those not directly responsible for the financial operations of the Army in the field, where the ultimate test of currency control would occur.

After the war began, the Army faced many new and pressing fiscal responsibilities. Finance sections had to plunge into their work, regardless of insufficient training and the lack of any existing coherent program for currency control. Other responsibilities, such as paying troops and commercial bills and exchanging foreign currencies, demanded immediate attention. There was hardly time to be systematic in trying to formulate control practices when other duties were more basic and when higher echelons seemed unaware of or uninterested in the matter. As the multiform fiscal activities developed, finance officers usually were too pressed to think systematically about the best methods of achieving control. Their actions were determined by the pressures of the moment, and without any logical, orderly plan having been formulated by the War Department, they improvised as best they could. The implication of such improvisations was that by the time an attempt was made to institute uniform controls, ingrained habits, practices, and attitudes often frustrated the attempt.

Although the Army never entirely comprehended the scope of its currency control problem, the need for some kind of currency control was understood. It realized that exchanges of pay in excess of disbursements would result in overdrafts, but this was never translated into effective controls. Even the controls it chose to employ were not uniformly applicable. Controls sometimes had to be altered to meet the demands of particular geographical areas, although the basic objective of limiting exchanges to disbursements prevailed in all overseas commands. The objectives were formulated for the parts of the globe where the need for currency control was great, as it was in Europe. A flourishing black market there offered lucrative inducements to violators of currency control. Most overseas operations, such as those in the southwest Pacific (Australia), India, and Hawaii, shared the European currency control objectives. In other locations currency control practices differed to the extent that troops were paid in dollars. Such payments did not mean that the Army's basic currency control objectives had changed; they merely meant that local conditions warranted some alterations in practice.

The currency control objectives in most areas were fourfold: to keep American currency away from the economies of friendly nations; to keep it inaccessible to Axis powers; to keep American servicemen from dealing in foreign black markets; and to keep any black-market profits (correctly assuming that despite all efforts, soldiers would be involved in black markets) from becoming claims on appropriated funds.

The first objective anticipated the power of the American dollar in relation to foreign currencies. The economies of most countries in combat theaters were directly and adversely affected by the war. Military demands for agricultural products and manufactured goods drastically reduced the amount of these items available for civilian consumption. Frequently, combat operations further reduced production by destroying factories or ruining farm lands. The resultant scarcity of goods was an automatic cause for inflation. If the Army had introduced the dollar, which had appreciated because of the inflation of foreign currencies, into these disrupted economies, it was manifest that other currencies could not compete equally. The other currencies would have naturally depreciated even further. The combination of the relatively stable position of the American dollar and the strained economies made it advisable to deal in local currencies. In this way, both the Army and the local populations would benefit, for prices would be controlled better for both. The United States government, in not disrupting economies, would also be fulfilling a moral obligation to other governments.[4]

Another currency control objective was predicated upon a desire to protect the integrity of the dollar. American currency could have been used to finance espionage activities, therefore the need to keep it inaccessible to Axis powers was clear. For this reason, the Army was obligated not to use standard American dollars in operations where substantial sums could have found their way into enemy coffers. Had the Army used dollars in areas where there was close contact with the enemy, some dollars would have inevitably found their way into local economies through soldier spending. This would have made it easy for the Axis powers to expend supplies of dollars they had acquired through hoarding before the war and through looting in countries they had conquered. The purchase of local collaboration would have been a particularly profitable use of dollars. In addition, a free use of dollars in overseas areas would have simplified for the enemy the acquisition of American bills to pay for espionage in the United States.

To keep American soldiers from dealing in foreign black markets was the third objective of currency control. Had soldiers been paid in dollars, they would have had an advantage because of the power of their currency in any black-market dealings. The Army thought that by disbursing local currencies, establishing exchange controls, and devising strict punitive measures for those caught violating the code, it was doing as much as possible to discourage soldiers in the black market.

The Army wanted to prevent any black-market profits from becoming claims on appropriated funds. This was a frankly realistic, but never attained goal because the Army usually chose the path of expediency over rigorous restrictions on exchanges. Although it tried to keep its personnel out of the black market, it realized that no amount of persuasion would deter the enterprising instincts of some officers and enlisted men. The Army could have prevented illicit profits from becoming claims on appropriated funds by limiting exchanges to amounts equal to pay and allowances, which were, of course, derived from appropriations. Obviously, the obligation of the government to exchange local currencies extended only to such amounts. Any currency exchanged in excess of these amounts represented a claim on the Treasury for which there was no appropriated money. This caused an overdraft—a condition the Army referred to as a "long position." That the overdraft ultimately amounted to $530,775,440 is eloquent testimony to the ineffectiveness of the Army's currency control.[5]

One of the complicating factors of currency control was that its objectives could not be applied on a worldwide basis. In three

particular areas—the South Pacific, China, and North Africa—
local conditions demanded a departure from the norm of disbursing local currencies. Operations in the South Pacific offered the
Army its choicest opportunity to use dollars, for there simply was
little need for employing local currencies in that area. Most island
economies were so underdeveloped that *any* soldier spending would
have been disruptive. Therefore, the American dollar was no more
injurious than any other currency would have been. Primitive economies likewise offered little opportunity for a black market. An
exception to this generalization was New Zealand which was not
primitive despite its agricultural economy. The possibility of the
Japanese capturing any large sum of money on South Pacific islands
was not a deterrent to the use of dollars because they would have
had no more opportunity to spend them locally than American soldiers had.

The War Department's decision to use dollars in China recognized the instability of the wartime Chinese economy. It would
have been grossly unfair to have paid soldiers in Chinese National
currency at the official rate of exchange, because their purchasing
power would have been cut drastically.[6] Although the Army flouted
all four objectives of currency control in China, it realized the im-
possibility of reforming Chinese economic conditions. Rather than
try to protect an economy already ruined or to interfere with a
black market tantamount to a national pastime, the Army was
wisely content to look after its own. The use of American currency
was justifiable since the amount of dollars disbursed in China could
not have materially affected the already wrecked Chinese economy.
American troops also were able to get the realistic purchasing
power of their dollars when they exchanged them at the black-
market rates.

In North Africa the Army used a special kind of American
dollar, the yellow seal dollar, purely as an expedient. These dollars
were distinguished from ordinary American bills by having the
Treasury Department seal printed in yellow rather than blue. When
the War Department was making plans for the North African invasion, it did not know what kind of cooperation it could expect
from the French provisional government. The Army decided to use
yellow seal dollars in the early phase of the operations rather than
run the risk of planning to use francs and then not being able to

get them in sufficient quantities. Since these dollars could be easily distinguished from the standard blue seal dollars, the entire series could have been declared nonlegal tender if any appreciable number fell into Axis hands.[7] After the position of the French government in North Africa became clear, the Army would make a further decision about the currency it would use. Presumably, if the French government joined the Allied cause, it would furnish francs to the American forces and there would be no further use of yellow seal dollars. Although the French government did join the Allies and did furnish francs, the Army never entirely abandoned yellow seal dollars in North Africa.

During hostilities, the War Department thought it had achieved the solution to the problem of currency control by using local currencies. As late as January, 1945, it had a totally uncritical attitude toward its system. In that month the War Department, in conjunction with the Treasury Department, stated that paying in local currencies "avoids the *possibility* [italics mine] that our soldiers might participate in illegal currency transactions." Army facilities for exchange, the statement continued, precluded the danger of "soldiers succumbing to the temptations of engaging in currency speculation with consequent damage to Army morale and efficiency as well as to the economy of the country where our troops may be stationed." [8] Subsequent experience was to prove that the faith of both the Army and Treasury in the efficacy of the program was entirely unfounded. But while the fighting continued, there was no vigorous test of the Army's system. Military operations focused the attention of most soldiers on their duties so that there was comparatively little time to indulge in currency speculation. Likewise, commanders were far more concerned with tactical considerations than with the black market, and appropriately so. Only after combat ceased was the Army able to see that its currency control problems had their genesis in the wartime system.

Although the War Department thought the use of local currencies would circumvent speculation, it did recognize the need to prevent inflation in areas where troops were increasing the amount of currency in circulation. Many finance officers advocated restricting pay in combat areas as the simplest means of currency control, but the Army chose not to impose any limitation on the percentage of pay a soldier could draw. The Army's judge advocate general declared that any compulsory withholding of pay would be contrary to law,[9] and the Army was loath to ask Congress for legislation permitting restricted payments.[10] As a consequence, the Army promoted a vigorous savings program as the most effective means at its disposal for channeling surplus pay away from foreign economies back to the States. Servicemen could establish dollar credits in the United States through the various types of savings available to them. Methods offered by the Army for saving money, in addition to those previously mentioned, included insurance programs and dependency allotments.

Early in the war the British were quick to recognize the dangers of large amounts of American money in the United Kingdom. The difference between the purchasing power of American soldiers and of the civilian population was a source of friction. British citizens resented the competition of American soldiers' money for the scarce items in their markets, and the Manchester *Guardian* complained that the buying power of American soldiers created a shortage of services and unrationed goods for British soldiers and civilians. This august newspaper advocated editorially that the cash available to American soldiers in Great Britain be regulated so as to approximate the amounts available to British troops.[11] This problem attracted the attention of President Franklin D. Roosevelt, who corresponded about the situation with John G. Winant, the American ambassador to the Court of St. James. The War Department and General Dwight D. Eisenhower, the European theater commander, also communicated frequently,[12] but the problem was never entirely solved.

The effect of soldier spending on the Australian economy was likewise a concern of the War Department. As early as November, 1942, the desirability of restricting funds in the hands of American soldiers in the Australian command, the southwest Pacific area, had been suggested by the War Department. The theater countered that there was no reason to limit soldiers' pay, because no competition existed between soldiers and civilians for consumer goods in Australia, as it did in England. Critical items were rationed; therefore, soldiers were subject to the general limitations. The theater thought that any effort to control the disposition of American soldiers' "modest salaries" would result in a sense of dissatisfaction and unfairness that would react unfavorably on the war effort. The attitude of the theater commandant, General Douglas MacArthur, was that if any effort were "to be made to equalize the pay of Allied soldiers, it should be made along the lines of raising the pay of soldiers of those countries that now receive less than the United States Army." [13]

General MacArthur's reply to the War Department's suggestion was that no inflationary trend could be attributed to his soldiers. At the same time, he wrote a letter to the Australian prime minister, the Right Honorable John Curtin, explaining with statistics how American troop spending could not be adversely affecting the Australian economy. During the six-month period from January 1 through June 30, 1944, 45 per cent of the total pay of southwest Pacific area personnel remained in the United States as allotments. This sum amounted to approximately $105,700,000. Twenty-six per cent ($61,100,000) was remitted back to the states in personal transfer accounts or money orders. Soldiers' deposits accounted for $7,650,000 or 3 per cent. Two per cent of the soldiers' pay, amounting to $4,300,000, went for cash purchases of war bonds and postage stamps. A substantial amount was also spent in post exchanges and other official channels; hence only a negligible portion of the Army's pay was circulated in the Australian economy.[14]

Since the Army was restrained from arbitrarily limiting the amount of pay a soldier could receive overseas, it activated its savings program. Participation in the program was supposed to be voluntary, because the Army had no more legal right to force a man to put his money in savings than it did to limit the amount of his pay he could receive. The chief finance officer of the European theater promoted a savings plan which stressed two points: the benefit to the individual saver and the benefit to the British economy.

The effect of the emphasis on savings can be seen in the following statistics. In May, 1943, the amount of pay retained by the individual in the European theater represented 57.7 per cent of his gross pay.[15] After the savings program was instituted, the average monthly percentage of pay retained by troops in the advance section of the theater's communications zone (support area to the rear of the fighting) from June, 1944, through April, 1945, fell to 14.5 per cent.[16] The Mediterranean theater's system of voluntary savings appeared to be as effective as that of the European theater. From July, 1944, through June, 1945, the monthly average of pay retained in Italy was 17.23 per cent.[17] And, as noted previously, in Australia from January 1 through June 30, 1944, only 24 per cent of the soldiers' pay remained to be spent on the local economy.[18]

Similarly, the vigorous efforts of the savings promotion officer of the China–Burma–India theater did not go unrewarded. In August, 1944, 75.5 per cent of the theater's total pay was returned through official channels, although in the following November, the figure was 80.6 per cent. The dollar difference was $995,324. During this period, the purchase of war bonds for cash and by Class "B" allotments increased 9.2 per cent. Twenty per cent more money was put into soldier's deposits. The reduction of the spending money left in the hands of troops from 24.5 per cent to 19.4 per cent was the equivalent of approximately 3,300,000 rupees.[19] The China theater also had remarkable success with its savings program in 1945.[20] More than 90 per cent of the pay and allowances disbursed in that command was either returned to the United States or spent in official channels. A popular form of savings in China was the $10 "GI" war bond, which could be bought at any finance office for cash.[21]

As commendable as the War Department's efforts were to promote savings campaigns in overseas theaters, the basic objectives of the currency control program transcended the effect of the savings program. Certainly this program achieved a notable accomplishment in reducing the percentage of pay retained overseas, benefiting both individual savers and foreign economies. But as long as loopholes existed which permitted soldiers to convert foreign currencies other than pay into dollar credits, the savings program was merely a palliative.

Chapter 2

Wartime Practices:
Foundation for Failure

IN most overseas areas problems of currency control developed despite the active savings program promoted by the War Department. These problems were not of a uniform nature; variations resulted from differing areas, economies, peoples, and currency control practices. For instance, the difficulties in China were entirely dissimilar to those on Pacific islands, and those in England bore a marked contrast to those of North Africa. In some locations the problems were strictly those of speculation and black-market profiteering, but in others they were confined to unsettling local economies. Although no one area had a monopoly on illicit currency transactions, they seemed to abound in those places where the standards of living were low. In China, North Africa, and Italy, Army black-market operators met little difficulty in collaborating with natives to gain a profit. The battleground areas of France and Germany also were fertile fields. There the very struggle for existence increased the willingness of people to do almost anything to survive, and conventional standards of western morality were swept away by the tidal wave of war.

The currency control difficulty on the islands of the middle Pacific was not the type of money used but the amount available for soldier spending. Since the presence of an Army unit on an island would mean more money in circulation than most island economies had previously experienced, efforts had to be directed toward minimizing funds available to soldiers. Even a minimal amount was likely to play havoc with primitive economies. From this standpoint, the problem was well-nigh insoluble. Military necessity dictated the use of the islands; their utility could not be foregone because soldier spending might wreck their economies. This was a situation where tactical considerations rightly took precedence over an administrative matter. The use of dollars in Hawaii caused no difficulty, because the dollar was the standard medium of exchange in the islands. Although the Hawaiian economy was somewhat inflated by the war, it was controlled rather carefully and was able, by and large, to withstand the shock of servicemen's dollars.

On June 25, 1942, the Hawaiian overstamp dollars became the only legal tender in the Hawaiian Archipelago. This special series was adopted as part of a scorched earth policy. At the time the American government could not determine whether a Japanese invasion of Hawaii was imminent. In case such an invasion occurred and the enemy gained control of the islands, the government did not want the Japanese to come into possession of any large amount of United States dollars. By using the Hawaiian series, the problem was solved. If the islands were conquered, the entire series could be declared nonlegal tender; Hawaiian dollars would thereby become worthless to any holder.[1]

Subsequent to the introduction of the Hawaiian overstamp series on June 25, 1942, the principal currency control challenge in the Territory of Hawaii was keeping standard American dollars out of circulation. The Army insisted that all its members use the Hawaiian dollars exclusively and provided complete facilities for exchanging currencies, but it received little cooperation from the Navy. With the introduction of Hawaiian dollars in June, 1942, the Navy exempted its personnel from having to use Hawaiian dollars, reasoning that sailors, as transients, should not be subjected to the same restrictions governing ground forces. Following suit, the Seventh Air Force requested the same privilege because its men were often on transient status. Any exemption from the control regulations obviously confuted their intent, since any servicemen using standard dollars in Hawaii could be identified as transients.[2]

Furthermore, the number of transients in the area could easily have been an indication of forthcoming tactical movements.

As American forces became victorious in the Pacific, Hawaiian dollars were employed in many operations. Once the armed forces started rolling back the Japanese, the Army seemed to have no fear that the enemy would recoup any of its losses. At least, any fear they might have had was not a deterrent to using both standard and overstamp dollars in the island operations. As early as 1942 standard dollars were being used to pay troops on Guadalcanal.[3] Throughout the war the South Pacific area used standard dollars. In the central and middle Pacific commands, the Hawaiian dollars were commonly disbursed.[4]

Reports differed on the currency control problem on Pacific islands depending on the point of view adopted. From the Army's position, little administrative difficulty was encountered, but from the islands' standpoint, trouble abounded because of the unprecedented introduction of money into their underdeveloped economies. These views are well exemplified by statements from the wartime fiscal director for the South Pacific area and the civil affairs officer on Tonga. The fiscal director, Colonel B. J. Tullington, contended that his command had no currency control problem because the islands' primitive economies offered soldiers a paucity of items for purchase. The only local product for which much demand existed was copra. Because of the lack of local outlets for their money, soldiers in the South Pacific usually returned through official channels from 75 to 90 per cent of the money they received.[5]

The civil affairs officer's report stated that since island economies were primitive, they were especially likely to be disrupted by even moderate soldier spending. The effect of soldiers arriving on Tonga was thought to be disastrous in the long run to the island's economic life. Servicemen who had been pent-up aboard ship a long time had both money and energy to spend when they landed. By paying fancy prices for coconuts, they reduced the islanders' incentive to produce copra. When American soldiers first arrived on Tonga in May, 1942, copra production dropped 80 per cent, and coconut planting stopped altogether. When troops paid three to four times the worth of bananas, banana exports dwindled by half. Tongans could sell trinkets for four times their value, and those who owned bicycles or horses rented them for as much as a dollar an hour, whereas the prewar rate had been fifty cents per day. Natives found it much easier to make money from soldiers than to work in their usual pursuits. Many "simply walked off their jobs to gather dollars more easily on the roadside." Some military authorities expressed the fear that Tongans would starve after the soldiers left, since they had forsaken their ordinary economic pursuits.[6]

The Okinawa campaign was unique among the Army's overseas operations from the standpoint of realistic currency control. Disregarding the War Department's injunction that withholding earned pay from soldiers was contrary to law, the Tenth Army interpreted the directive of the United States Army Forces, Pacific Ocean Areas (USAFPOA), that firm currency control be maintained on Okinawa as a license for restricting pay. Since the Tenth Army decided that no post exchanges would operate in the Ryukyus Islands until sixty days after the landing, it declared that troops would have no use for their pay. Consequently, it took the following steps to limit money in the hands of soldiers: (1) No payments were made until the end of May, 1945—two months after the invasion began. (2) Maximum partial payments of $25 in yen for enlisted men were scheduled for the May payday with the exact amount to be determined by the quantity of merchandise available for purchase. As it turned out, funding difficulties precluded even this payment. (3) In the month of June, soldiers on Okinawa were to have been paid $40 in yen, but they actually received only $10. (4) When pay accounts were settled in full, unpaid amounts were converted into some form of savings. Soldiers had an option on what form of savings they would use, but they enjoyed no option between drawing cash or saving their funds.[7]

Wartime problems of currency control in China were comparatively slight. If the standard currency control practices had been applied there, this condition would have been indeed paradoxical in view of the rampant Chinese black (or "free") market. However, the usual practices did not prevail. The first sizeable contingent of American soldiers arrived in southwest China in the spring of 1943, but the impact of their spending in local markets did not become noticeable until that autumn. From then on, American servicemen were an important source of dollars for China's money market.[8] Troops were paid in standard American dollars. They had the privilege of converting any amount of their pay into Chinese currency, but they could not exchange Chinese money for dollars or dollar credits. The reason for this no-exchange rule was that finance officers were not obligated to accept or exchange currency they had not disbursed. Therefore, the exchange mechanism in China was not a medium for converting black-market profits into dollar credits as it was in Europe.[9]

Although American troops in China were paid in American dollars, the Army needed Chinese National currency (CNC)—as distinguished from currencies introduced into China by Japanese puppet governments, Central Reserve Bank notes (CRB) and Federal Reserve Bank notes (FRB)—for various housekeeping and procurement purposes. Previous to February, 1944, the United States government had been buying Chinese National currency from the Chinese government at the official rate of exchange, $5.125 (US) for $100 (CNC), commonly known as the 20-to-1 rate. The tremendous inflation in wartime China and the fluctuation in the black-market value of the American dollar made this 20-to-1 rate ridiculous,[10] but the Chinese government preferred to maintain the fiction of this ratio, finding it "inadvisable to chase the black market rate endlessly." [11] Furthermore, this fantastic overvaluation of the currency enabled the Chinese government to achieve the desired Oriental goal of saving face. As documentation for the extreme currency inflation in China during the war, one source gives the following figures for the free-market exchange rate between Chinese National currency dollars and the American dollar: [12]

1941	June	19:1	1944	June	192:1
	December	18.93:1		December	570:1
1943	June	59:1	1945	June	1705:1
	December	84:1		December	2185:1

Realizing that the Chinese economy would be unstable for an indefinite time period, the United States government persuaded the Chinese to agree to abandoning the 20-to-1 ratio in official transactions. In February, 1944, the two governments came to an understanding whereby the Chinese would furnish all the currency needed by finance officers, with equitable settlements to be made quarterly. Since no exchange rate was placed upon these funds advanced by the Chinese, they were known as "no rate funds." On September 30, 1944, the War Department made a settlement with the Chinese government on all obligations in no rate funds incurred prior to that date. The amount of the settlement was $210,000,000.[13]

American soldiers in China wanting native currency for expenditures on local markets did not exchange their dollars for Chinese money at Army finance offices but went into the free market and made the transactions at the going rate. This was the only way they could receive equitable purchasing power with their money. Should they have been restricted to converting their dollars in official channels before the no rate exchange agreement was reached with the Chinese government, they would have received only a fraction of the value of their dollars because of the unrealistic ratio between the currencies. Although the War Department was reluctant to let soldiers get involved in the Chinese black market (and it did so with the knowledge of the State and Treasury departments), it realized that under the circumstances it had no other choice. The Army would have been faced with a grave morale problem if it had tried to restrict conversions to finance offices, where only the official rate of exchange could be used.[14]

Dollars that found their way into the Chinese black market inevitably became involved in speculations with other currencies. In 1943 a brisk trade developed between dollars and piastres at the border of China and French Indo-China because Japanese officials in occupied Indo-China were eager to purchase as many dollars as possible. Such eagerness might have indicated a lack of confidence in their ultimate victory and a concomitant lowering of morale, but more probably it was merely a recognition of the dollar as a powerful trading medium. A black-market operator who could get dollars to the border might have made a fivefold profit. The border rate of exchange was $1.00 (US) to 10 piastres. One piastre brought $25 (CNC) on the Kunming black market. If a speculator exchanged $1.00 (US) for 10 piastres on the border and then brought his piastres to Kunming, he could exchange them for $250 (CNC). Assuming that $50 (CNC) would buy one American dollar (a sanguine assumption, even for early 1943), the $250 (CNC) derived from the exchange of piastres could then be converted into $5.00 (US). Thus the $1.00 (US) which began the series of transactions at the border could be parlayed into $5.00 (US) in Kunming.[15]

Soldiers were not allowed to profiteer by exchanging Chinese currency for dollars in official channels, but they were obviously not without the means of turning a profit in the black market, as the dollar-piastre transaction illustrates. China Clearing Board dollar drafts offered a further opportunity for currency speculation. The China Clearing Board was an organization for handling monetary problems of American missionaries in China. It had a bank account with the National City Bank of New York, to which missionaries' churches deposited dollars.

Before June, 1944, missionaries in China had been forced to exchange their dollars at the official rate of exchange. Although they were "seriously embarrassed" by using the official rate, the nature of their calling was a deterrent to extralegal fiscal transactions. In June, 1944, the board made an arrangement with the Chinese government whereby it could sell dollar drafts on its New York bank account in the open market. The dollar drafts sold for 100 to 110 yuan to the dollar. Soldiers, who were able to exchange their dollars for around 200 yuan to the dollar, bought these missionaries' dollar drafts at the rate of about 100 yuan to the dollar, thereby having a potential profit of 100 per cent. They would then mail these drafts to relatives or friends in the United States who would cash them. The possibility existed for the proceeds to be returned to soldiers in China by postal money order, thus permitting a repetition of the profitable transaction.

Since no official United States funds were involved in these speculations, the Army was in no position to lose. It was concerned, however, because the speculation not only diverted attention from military duties, but more important because it increased the demand for dollars with which to buy bank drafts. Soldiers canceled allotments so they could draw a maximum number of dollars across the pay table. This desire for dollars had serious logistical implications, for currency had to be flown across the Hump. The Treasury Department also expressed some perturbation over soldiers' speculations in China and even considered asking the China Clearing Board to quit selling drafts directly to soldiers because of the unfavorable reaction of the Chinese government. During July, 1944,

Army personnel bought $400,000 in China Clearing Board drafts. Most men bought drafts for $1,000 to $2,000, but some went as high as $10,000. This bonanza played out in September, 1944, when members of the Army were prohibited from any traffic in dollar drafts.[16]

The situation in the British Isles was quite different from that of China because the extensiveness of a black market was largely dependent upon the natives' attitude toward extralegal dealings. The British people never permitted the development of wholesale black markets such as those found in France, Germany, and China. They were willing to stand to the end as a nation-in-arms, and less willing than residents of other war-torn countries to see their sense of public integrity sullied. This spirit of determination was perhaps best expressed by Prime Minister Winston Churchill when he said, "We shall fight on the beaches, we shall fight on the landing grounds, we shall fight in the fields and in the streets, we shall fight in the hills; we shall never surrender." [17] After the war the British further displayed their national economic integrity by subscribing to the austerity program; France, on the other hand, chose the easier path of unregulated inflation. The great suffering inflicted on the English people by the Nazi blitz provided little inducement for their turning to a black market for scarce items. Because Britishers were willing to endure shortages or combat them in the queue, the few discovered breaches of currency control in the United Kingdom were largely the result of manipulations by American soldiers. In April, 1943, cases of American servicemen dealing illegally in British currencies were brought to light. Flyers were transporting currencies out of England to money markets where they could profit on exchanges. When these violators were identified, they were disciplined.[18]

The prime factor making currency control difficult in the Mediterranean area was the use of American currency. Initially, the Army employed blue seal dollars in North Africa; and throughout the war in countries bordering on the Mediterranean, it used yellow seal currency as an expedient, along with such notes as the Allied military lire and francs of the French provisional government. Such expediency emphasized the makeshift quality and weakness of the Army's currency control program. The very use of dollars was an invitation to difficulties, and additional factors were also operating to defeat control. Among them was the eagerness of North Africans to enter illicit financial dealings—an eagerness which no doubt found its equal in American servicemen. North Africa further presented a rewarding field for currency speculation because there was always a large number of transients in the area. With the constant movement of personnel, currency control assumed formidable dimensions.

In Egypt, where American forces were paid in yellow seal dollars—as elsewhere in North Africa—the Army was confronted with something of a dilemma. Obviously, soldiers would spend their dollars in the local markets, and this money would find its way into the normal Egyptian commercial channels. The Army had a policy of purchasing American currency from local banks, thus reducing logistical burdens.[19] At the same time, it was apprehensive about large-scale transactions in dollars, since it was clearly acquiring dollars far in excess of those disbursed as troop pay. In entering such commercial negotiations, the Army feared it might be playing into the hands of international currency syndicates; furthermore, there was always the possibility that Axis agents were involved, either by unloading hoarded American currency or by purchasing more dollars for espionage.

By December, 1944, the finance officer of the Cairo military district had purchased a total of $3,049,676 in yellow seal dollars from the National Bank of Egypt. Such a sum was obviously suspect. But because Egypt was not an occupied territory, the American Army could exercise no control over civilians and commercial firms, regardless of their dealings in United States currency. All the theater (United States Army Forces in the Middle East) could do in buying dollars from the Egyptian bank was to follow the advice of the Army Service Forces fiscal director. Further negotiations were left to the American State and Treasury departments and the Egyptian government.[20]

Although Egyptians might have been implicated in questionable transactions involving millions of yellow seal dollars, they were not the sole currency manipulators. Some American soldiers tried to profit from exchanges in local markets by trading their money locally for more francs and lire than they could get at Army disbursing offices, then returning the money to a finance office for redemption. Since the official exchange rate prescribed less francs and lire to the dollar than the soldiers had received on the local market, they would show a net dollar gain. When caught trying to profit at the Army's expense, they were turned over to the provost marshal for disciplinary action.[21]

The finance department, as the agency through which currency exchanges were handled, was thought to be above suspicion in matters of illicit currency speculation. Thus it was particularly noticeable when a finance man was caught in an illegal transaction. A sergeant who was the cashier for a finance section in Egypt established the unit's bank account in his own name in September, 1944. Accounts had previously been set up by mistake in individual's names in the Egyptian branches of Barclay's Bank; therefore, when Barclay's Heliopolis branch reported the instance to the theater fiscal director, it presumed it was only correcting a mistake similar to earlier ones. During investigation, it developed that the sergeant had not only erred in establishing the account incorrectly but had also been using his position as cashier to employ government funds to finance currency speculation. With Egyptian pounds he would buy large amounts of francs and lire from money changers at rates lower (more francs and lire per pound) than the official Army rates of exchange; then he would return to the finance office and exchange his francs and lire at the more advantageous rate for Egyptian pounds. After the cashier's manipulations were discovered, he was brought before a court martial.[22]

The constant movement of troops in the Mediterranean area posed major currency control difficulties. Whether soldiers were moving across the Mediterranean from North Africa to Italy, from Cairo to Tripoli, or from Naples to the United States, the factor of currency speculation was omnipresent. An important leakage occurred when troops were deploying from the Mediterranean to the United States. In August, 1944, a considerable traffic in desirable blue seal dollars arose in Naples due to the sometimes unavoidable delay between the time troops received travel orders and the time they sailed. Deploying soldiers were supposed to exchange their lire for blue seal dollars, and this time lag gave them the opportunity to make more than one exchange on the same travel order. They could take their blue seal dollars into the Naples black market and trade them for lire at a ratio much higher than the official rate of exchange; then they could take their bounty to a finance office and get it converted into dollars at the official rate, thereby making a tidy profit. Violators stood the best chance of succeeding with their scheme if they took their travel orders to a different finance office for each exchange because risk of detection was not great with the large volume of business in port areas. Soldiers could also use their travel orders to exchange lire for friends.[23] Similar leakages occurred when American troops were leaving Oran, Algeria, for the United States. To curtail such activity, the commanding general of the Mediterranean base section proposed that only a small amount of dollars be given departing soldiers. The sum should be barely sufficient to cover purchases on shipboard, and any remainder due them would be given in Treasury checks.[24]

Instances of American dollars being sought by natives were frequent in all North Africa. In Casablanca soldiers had many outlets for selling yellow seal dollars for a substantial premium in French currency. One merchant paid a soldier 28 per cent above the legal exchange rate for dollars and told him that he would pay the same rate for all dollars brought to him. In some places premiums ran as high as 160 per cent. Arab shoeshine boys, who began by dealing in black-market American goods, by 1944 had developed into accomplished financiers. They, too, drained American currency away from legal channels by paying premiums for it. One reason why natives and refugees hoarded yellow seal dollars was that they had more confidence in the stability of dollars than in French francs—an example of Gresham's law in operation. Nazi agents, who preferred to purchase blue seal dollars for espionage purposes, turned to the yellow seal when the others became unobtainable, contributing further to the drain on American bills.[25]

The laxity of French law was still another factor making the black market in yellow seal dollars difficult to control. In French North Africa it was not illegal for anyone to purchase property of the American government so long as he declared it for customs purposes and paid duty on it. Hence, an African possessor of any American property could not be punished. Before the seller could be arrested, he had to be caught in the act of selling government property to natives. French authorities actually encouraged such transactions by allowing merchants to enter port areas where they made their arrangements.[26]

Port areas were sore spots for currency control because American merchant seamen were the most active black-market offenders. Due to their accessibility to goods and wide range of contacts, merchant seamen made great profits in the black market in the Mediterranean area. When seamen entered a port, they were not allowed outside the dock area until they converted all their dollars into local currency and had a certificate to that effect. Then, as they were preparing to sail, they could exchange back into dollars only the amount shown on the certificate, plus any pay advances they might have received while ashore. These advances had to be certified by a war shipping administration agent.[27]

Obviously, when the American military commands in the Mediterranean area allowed merchant seamen to reconvert into dollars the total sum of native currency taken ashore, they were making no allowances for normal living expenses. This meant that the mariners could live off the black market their entire time in port. By taking a marketable item into the Persian Gulf command and selling it for rials, a seaman could indulge in the Persian fleshpots and still reconvert his remaining rials into dollars, up to the limit of his original amount. Thus, he compensated for his shore expenses with black-market profits. Although some profits were inevitably translated into dollars in this manner, any kind of exchange regulation trying to incorporate a living expense differential would undoubtedly have been administratively infeasible.

On the other hand, most merchant seamen probably were not content to limit their black-market profits to what they could spend in living ashore. Since they were involved in illicit transactions to make money, not merely to live in style for brief periods, they usually demanded payment in yellow seal dollars for goods sold in port areas. Reconversion regulations limited the amount of rials or lire a mariner could exchange to the dollar equivalent he had taken ashore but did not prevent sailors from bringing dollars back on board. Although native black marketeers hated to part with their American currency, the seamen were usually successful in demanding their own terms, for the natives knew they could make handsome resale profits on goods bought from Americans. The seamen experienced no trouble exchanging yellow for blue seal currency when they returned to the United States.[28]

Accompanying the great decrease in the supply of dollar bills in North Africa was the total disappearance of the American coins with which soldiers had been paid immediately after the invasion. Payments at that time were made half in bills and half in specie. Unlettered natives, who immediately assumed the coins to be of greater stability than the paper, made particular efforts to acquire them. They also preferred coins because of the unusually short life of bills caused by North African climatic conditions.[29]

On one occasion American soldiers in North Africa were able to profit on currency transactions without getting involved in the black market—a situation which brought into focus the inconsistency and unreality of wartime currency control. This unusual opportunity developed when Army post offices and finance offices were operating simultaneously with different rates of exchange. The initial rate of exchange between francs and dollars in North Africa was 75-to-1. The Treasury Department thought this ratio "fair and generous." It was, however, prepared to accept the rate of 50-to-1 if the French Committee of National Liberation insisted that the latter rate was to the best French interests.[30] President Roosevelt and Prime Minister Churchill agreed to the French desire for the increased rate at the Casablanca Conference in February, 1943, and the 75-to-1 rate of exchange was abandoned throughout North and West Africa.[31]

On February 2, 1943, all Army post offices began using the 50-to-1 exchange rate. But military personnel could exchange yellow seal dollars at the 75-to-1 rate at banks through February 8 and at Army finance offices through February 15! All a soldier had to do to take advantage of this boon was exchange his yellow seal dollars for francs at 75-to-1 at a finance office; then go directly to an Army post office and buy money orders to send to the States at the 50-to-1 rate. As if troops would not use their ingenuity to produce a maximum number of yellow seal dollars in order to take advantage of this 50 per cent profit, finance officers were permitted to settle arrears in pay earned through January 31 at the 75-to-1 rate as late as August 31, 1943, provided they had the authorization of the chief finance officer of the Allied Forces Headquarters (AFHQ).[32]

Although the Mediterranean area had many transients and abounded in seaports which were especially conducive to black-marketing, there were fewer currency control problems than in most overseas commands, according to the theater's deputy fiscal director, Captain (later Lieutenant Colonel) T. W. Archer. The Mediterranean theater's formula for ensuring currency control was to charge finance officers with the responsibility for transmitting no more money back to the States than they had disbursed. This system eliminated the need for imposing any elaborate regulatory system on the troops or for trying to regulate the actions of each soldier.

In fact, it was the Mediterranean theater's policy to place a minimal restriction on the individual. Soldiers going on leave to any Italian city were not encumbered with certificates stating the amount of currency in their possession when leaving their organization. "Men coming out of the line for a week's rest leave in Rome and who would be returning to the front at the end of the week didn't give a damn about currency control!" declared the deputy fiscal director. "Any attempt to place restrictions on the individual under such circumstances would have been useless." If disbursing officers kept a rigid control over transmissions back to the States, soldiers could not profit at the American government's expense, regardless of how wide a swath they cut in the Italian black market. Such a policy certainly did little, however, to help the Italian government fight its own battles against inflation.

As one means of preventing black-market profits from being channeled through finance offices, the Mediterranean theater ruled that only 50-lire notes and lower could be exchanged—a stumbling block for many would-be profiteers. One instance concerned a soldier who captured a German truck carrying Italian currency north of Milan. The bills he looted were all large, and he exchanged them for 50-lire notes. When he got to a finance office south of Rome, he presented the entire amount for transmission back to the States as a personal transfer account. Since such an enormous sum obviously could not have been derived from pay and allowances, the finance officer called the provost marshal to come pick up a likely black marketeer. The finance officer confiscated the lire, but the provost marshal did not punish the soldier since he had captured the funds and not acquired them in the black market. This example was typical of the Mediterranean theater's procedure. Any time that an individual appeared at a finance office in the theater trying to convert more than he had been paid, disbursing officers would summarily collect the surplus. In such cases, soldiers had no recourse. The authoritarian approach of the Mediterranean theater extended into all phases of currency control. It kept the troops' desire for yellow seal dollars to a minimum through a vigorous whispering campaign; rumors were circulated that the yellow seal would be nonconvertible in the United States. "Enough men were scared off," said the deputy fiscal director, "that we had little trouble." Of course, no amount of pressure or suggestion could keep some servicemen from trying to circumvent controls. One soldier was caught trying to mail yellow seal dollars home by tucking them inside the pages of *Stars and Stripes,* which normally was not censored. Each time an individual was caught in an illicit action, the theater gave wide publicity to the case, using the Army's common punitive technique of making an example of the offender.[33] After the Army made its final tabulations of the foreign currencies it had exchanged in excess of disbursements, it discovered a negligible overdraft in lire. This finding indicates that the Mediterranean theater's formula for currency control was largely successful, if unorthodox.

When the Allied forces invaded France, the operation was different in one notable respect from the earlier invasion of Italy. The Italian operation was against an enemy government, whereas the Normandy invasion of June 6, 1944, was to drive the Germans from the homelands of governments-in-exile with which the United States had maintained amicable relations. The policy, therefore, was not to use Allied military currencies, as had been done in Italy, but to make arrangements with the governments concerned for the advance production of special or supplementary issues of their national currencies. From the standpoint of currency control, though, there was one possible disadvantage in dealing with friendly governments: the United States government felt honor-bound to take into consideration the wishes of the friendly government in determining the exchange rate between the dollar and the foreign monetary unit. If an unrealistic exchange rate was agreed upon, whatever the political considerations, it produced patent currency control problems for the American Army. In France, where the exchange rate overvalued the franc, soldiers felt justified in entering the black market in an effort to realize some purchasing power on the French economy.

In planning the currency aspects of the Normandy invasion, the

United States government was eager to avoid a repetition of its World War I experience in France; consequently, it was happy to get the concurrence of the French Committee of National Liberation in having a special issue of supplementary franc notes printed in America. In World War I the staff of General John J. Pershing had waited until arriving in France before making an attempt to procure francs with which to pay troops and commercial bills. In a White House press conference shortly after the Normandy invasion, President Roosevelt stated that during World War I American soldiers in France were paid in dollars; furthermore, he said that a sizeable number of these dollars found their way under French mattresses and had been turning up for redemption ever since.[34] (However, the President's sly comment on wartime manners and morals was not based on fact, since dollars were not used in France.) Although the invasion of France did not occur until June, 1944, planning for the French supplemental currency began long before then. The Bureau of Engraving and Printing started printing the French bills around February 15, 1944.[35]

By early 1945, after the tide of battle had swept through France, the European theater began to realize that its currency control measures needed some tightening. The areas over which it became concerned were not those involved in combat operations at the time but, rather, rear areas such as France had become. While forces were engaged in battle, they had little time for currency speculation. Those soldiers in the support areas, on the other hand, found plenty of time to deal in the black market. They had access to post exchange goods, which they could sell to Continentals for inflated prices. Consequently, as long as finance offices were converting soldiers' foreign currency into dollar credits, a serviceman could easily make a profit.

In March, 1945, the European theater made its first move to halt the conversion of black-market profits into dollar credits. It published a directive stating that any person wanting to transmit funds to the United States by personal transfer account, postal money order, or war bonds had to first make application to his unit personnel officer, who was charged with keeping a record of each individual's pay and allowances and transmissions of funds to the States. If the amount presented for transmission home exceeded that available for transfer, as shown on the personnel officer's records, the application was denied. If a soldier were within his limits, the personnel officer countersigned the application, indicating that he had entered the transaction on his records. He then returned the application to the soldier, who processed it through the finance office or Army post office. Officers of field grade and above (majors, lieutenant colonels, colonels, and generals) were excluded from these restrictions. Such an exemption proved to be unwise for two reasons: it created much resentment and ill will on the part of company grade officers (lieutenants and captains) and enlisted men, and it excluded a group whose black-market activities were just as pronounced as those of the lesser ranks.[36]

In France, as well as in Italy, a minor problem was created by counterfeit currency. Usually wartime counterfeits were so imperfect that their recognition was not difficult, but there was always the possibility of their not being detected in the large volume of currency passing through finance offices. In December, 1944, when numerous reports of counterfeit francs in the Allied military authority series reached the European theater headquarters, all 500- and 1000-franc notes were withdrawn. Thereafter, only Banque de France francs in those denominations were legal tender. When the supplemental notes were withdrawn, soldiers could go to a finance office to exchange any 500- or 1000-franc Allied military authority note for the same denomination issued by the Banque de France.[37] Disbursing officers discovering any counterfeit bills collected them and obtained from the holders the circumstances of their coming into possession of the bogus money. All French counterfeit bills and intelligence reports were sent to the central disbursing officer in Paris. This information was forwarded to the United States Secret Service, which throughout the war was active in investigating foreign counterfeiting. The Secret Service worked together with military intelligence to trace Continental counterfeit rings.[38]

Although American soldiers quickly became involved with the German black market after they crossed that nation's border, they did not have quite so much opportunity for profiteering as troops in less active areas. Perhaps it is a credit to their Yankee ingenuity that they capitalized on their situation as much as they did. Their combat duties notwithstanding, soldiers began presenting reichsmarks for exchange in November, 1944. Presumably these reichsmarks were from the black market, since they were not issued as pay. To control currency, as far as the exchange of reichsmarks for dollar credits was concerned, the fiscal office of the communications zone's advance section prohibited disbursing officers under its jurisdiction from accepting further reichsmarks.[39]

Other segments of the European theater were not so realistic and stringent as the advance section: they allowed finance officers to accept reichsmarks that soldiers might have received as change in legitimate business transactions. Since the largest bill disbursed in the Allied occupation currency, Allied military marks, was the 100-mark denomination, 100-mark notes in the reichsmark or rentenmark series could not have been obtained as change and therefore were not acceptable. Other bills unacceptable in finance offices for the same reason were Belgian and French 1000-franc notes and Dutch 100-florin notes.[40] In reality *any* traffic in reichsmarks, a currency not disbursed to soldiers, invited a breakdown of currency control. That American soldiers, as individuals, had "legitimate" business dealings with Germans would be a difficult matter to substantiate, since all the necessities were provided by the Army.

In April, 1945, the European theater declared Allied military marks the only legal tender for official transactions. This decision to use Allied military marks exclusively in Army channels was a step toward simplifying control measures, since after the reichsmarks were banned, any soldier found possessing them could be investigated and disciplined.[41]

By V-E Day American soldiers had indulged in sufficient black-market currency speculation for the European theater fiscal director to recommend that a currency be adopted strictly for the payment of American servicemen. This could be used by them to remit funds to the United States, buy postal money orders, purchase war bonds, make deposits, or exchange for foreign currencies; but there would be no reconversion privilege.[42] Although the need was obvious, the European theater took no action at the end of hostilities to adopt scrip. The advice of the fiscal director was ignored—because the aligning of his functions with a subordinate echelon had made his position less influential.[43] If the Army had adopted his recommendation for a scrip currency it would have saved the United States government hundreds of millions of dollars.

Chapter 3

Wartime Policy-Making For Europe

THE previous chapter demonstrated that day-to-day operational decisions in overseas theaters lacked the consistency and logic necessary for a successful currency control program, but probably the greatest impediment to workable, effective controls was the indecision evident at the highest policy-making levels of the Army. A further stumbling block was the lack of centralized responsibility. With several different agencies, of many diverse interests and viewpoints, having a voice in policy-making, the result was that no agency could act with dispatch and assurance.

If the War Department appeared unaware of the consequences of its ineffective currency control policy toward the end of hostilities in Europe—and of the mammoth problems that would lie ahead—other agencies of the government anticipated the difficulties the Army might encounter. And in certain Army quarters there was an interest in the types of controls that would be necessary after the fighting ceased, but this appeared to be limited, for no general postwar policy was enunciated.

In April, 1944, the Treasury Department asked the War Department about its fiscal plans for occupied areas. Major General Arthur H. Carter, fiscal director of the Army Service Forces, indicated that the Army's savings program diverted enough money

31

away from overseas economies to obviate the need for a more stringent currency control. William H. Taylor, chief of the Treasury's division of monetary research, said the Treasury had no quarrel with the Army's past performance, but it wondered if the Army was looking ahead to the need for controls as additional territories were occupied. When Taylor asked the Army to consider the possibility of devising a system whereby a soldier could not remit to the States more than he had drawn in pay and allowances, General Carter countered that the whole subject of remittance procedures was being studied continuously.[1]

The Army's studying produced little in the way of concrete results, for in June, 1945, the Treasury was questioning the lack of control of excess remittances from Germany, realizing that the Army was still allowing its soldiers to transmit to the United States funds they had acquired in the black market.[2]

The War Department's studies during hostilities did not produce a workable solution for the occupation period because they were too narrow and stayed on the periphery of the problem. Instead of getting to the central issue, by devising means of limiting remittances to funds drawn through official channels, the department investigated particular violations of currency control. Among these was the misuse of postal money orders to remove black-market profits from an overseas area, money orders being a favorite device of speculators. But its efforts would have been much more effective had it strictly regulated the use of all transmission channels.[3]

If the War Department's planning for currency control was piecemeal, that of some overseas theaters was likewise limited. The first memorandum from the European theater fiscal director, Brigadier General Nicholas H. Cobbs, in September, 1944, dealing with German currencies failed to mention any need for exercising controls. It merely stated that reichsmarks and rentenmarks could be disbursed and collected by finance officers on an equal basis with Allied military marks.[4] This indicates that General Cobbs's thinking on the matter had gone little further than in 1942 when the office of the theater fiscal director was inaugurated. At that time the enumeration of the fiscal director's responsibilities omitted any specific reference to currency control per se.

On September 7, the very same day in 1944 that the European theater published its memorandum on German currencies, the

North African theater put out a circular on currency control. Whereas the European theater memorandum skirted the issue, the North African theater circular stated plainly that finance officers were to make no exchanges for individuals until they had signed certificates as to the legitimacy of the source of their funds.[5]

The most grievous collapse of currency control occurred in the European theater. The primary reasons for this failure were that more troops were in the European theater than in the Far East and that in Germany Americans contacted Russian soldiers who were injecting countless Allied military marks into the local economy. The European theater and the War Department were unprepared to meet the problems presented by occupied areas. The best illustration of the theater's reluctance to acknowledge the seriousness of the situation was their failure to carry through General Cobbs's desire in the spring of 1945 to restrict the use of certain currencies.

In March, 1945, the fiscal office of the communications zone's advance section accumulated $52,875.60 in reichsmarks and rentenmarks. These funds had been turned over by the First and Ninth Armies. Since these marks had been accepted by finance officers before the Roer crossing and since a non-fraternization policy was in effect in March, the marks had unmistakably come from illegal sources. The commanding general of the advance section recommended a prohibition against the acceptance by finance officers of indigenous marks, because their acquisition was unlawful and because the Army had an ample supply of Allied military marks.[6] His sentiments were echoed by the Third Army and the Twelfth Army Group. The Seventh Army went so far as to enact the prohibition without asking the concurrence of a superior headquarters.[7]

After the strong reaction of the field against illegal indigenous marks, General Cobbs drafted instructions to finance, postal, and post exchange officers to accept or issue no further reichsmarks. Before he dispatched his message, he circularized the draft among the theater staff. The assistant chief of staff for civil affairs and military government (G-5) of the Supreme Headquarters, Allied Expeditionary Forces (SHAEF) objected to the instructions because they would cause a disparity between the value of reichsmarks and Allied military marks, which would have been contrary to the intent of Military Government Law Number 51. In other words, G-5 was willing for the Army to accept illegally acquired currency to maintain the integrity of a military government law, but it was unwilling for the Army to protect itself financially by prohibiting the acceptance of funds it had not disbursed.[8]

The European theater G-1 (assistant chief of staff for personnel) analyzed General Cobbs's proposal more realistically than G-5. G-1 stated that by allowing soldiers to use reichsmarks, the European theater placed itself in the untenable position of denouncing all forms of black-market activity with provisions for disciplinary action for involvement therein at the same time it facilitated black-market dealings by accepting funds patently secured from unlawful sources. Therefore, G-1 concurred with the fiscal director on a general prohibition of the use of German indigenous currencies, G-5 of the supreme headquarters notwithstanding. G-1 said, "This matter is essentially one of fiscal, currency control, soldier savings, and discipline rather than of civil affairs." [9] This conclusion was approved by the European theater deputy chief of staff. On the authority of his approval, the fiscal director published the prohibition on April 19, 1945.[10] It was announced through all channels of communication in the command. A finance circular letter went directly to disbursing officers in Germany, stating that they would disburse Allied military marks only. The letter from the European theater adjutant general to commanding generals specified that only Allied military marks would be used for disbursements and other official transactions.[11]

The April 19 prohibition had not been published a month when repercussions began. Lieutenant General Walter Bedell Smith, the supreme headquarters chief of staff, informed the commanding general of the communications zone that the prohibition was "clearly a discrimination between Allied Military Marks and Reichsmarks and contravened the provisions of Military Government Law No. 51." He went on to say that the fiscal director had taken his action despite the expressed disapproval of the supreme headquarters G-5 and that the supreme headquarters had not been notified when the prohibition was published. General Smith requested an explanation of this unorthodox behavior.[12]

After communications zone headquarters received General Smith's request, it relayed the letter to the European theater G-1, who sent it down to General Cobbs for a reply. General Cobbs explained that the April 19 prohibition was published upon the approval of the European theater deputy chief of staff. Cobbs's justification of the prohibition in his proposed reply to the supreme commander contained a realistic analysis of the Army's currency control problem in occupied territories:

> The result of accepting indigenous German currency opened the gates for persons who had such currency illegally acquired, to increase their pay at the expense of the United States. Certainly it is better to protect the interest of our own government than that of a defeated enemy.
>
> I cannot agree that the action taken contravenes any provision of Military Government Law Number 51, as that was interpreted, and I think correctly, as governing the German people, and not the American Army in placing any restrictions necessary to protect the interests of the United States.
>
> The influence of this action in making the Germans suspicious of the value of the Reichsmark is negligible as the value of all German currency has collapsed in relation with other currencies, and for the United States to try to support it in relation to the Allied Military Mark at the expense of the United States would appear to be contrary to the best interests of the United States regardless of the effect on the German indigenous currency.[13]

The crucible of Continental operations had clearly developed in General Cobbs an intense awareness of the nature of the currency control challenge facing the Army. Although his earlier policy pronouncements did not indicate any real comprehension of currency control problems, it is to his credit that when the situation was dramatized, he did understand the implications. Others who should have developed similar understanding never did. Had the perceptiveness demonstrated by General Cobbs's statement prevailed in the War Department or at the supreme headquarters, the European theater's currency control program probably would have been much more successful.

Soon after the supreme headquarters had registered its disapproval of the April 19 prohibition, the War Department also took up the cudgel against the European theater offenders. On June 7, 1945, Major General George J. Richards, the War Department budget officer, radioed the theater's communications zone headquarters to ask if the offending prohibition had been rescinded.[14] Then on June 22 the Washington (Army Service Forces) Office of the Fiscal Director instructed the supreme headquarters that the prohibition should be removed.[15] Although the European theater never revoked the prohibition against indigenous marks, the matter became strictly academic in face of the flood of Allied military marks Russia poured into the German economy. When the Army should have been concerned with prohibiting the Russian-printed marks, it was devoting attention to reichsmarks—decidedly a side issue. The fact that approximately 80 per cent of the overdraft in marks was of Russian origin indicated that the Army tried to cope with the wrong offender.[16]

While the European theater controverted with higher echelons about the prohibition against indigenous marks, other discussions were occurring in the War Department that revealed similar misunderstandings of the currency control problems facing overseas theaters. Colonel Bernard Bernstein, chief of the supreme headquarters G-5 currency section, when confronted with the inflated German economy, outlined for the War Department a possible method of maintaining control of currency. He suggested that soldiers be credited with their full pay in the United States and in addition draw a monthly ration of marks, the amount being determined by current economic conditions. Soldiers would have no conversion privileges, since they would be protected against loss of pay by receiving full pay credits in the United States. The limited number of marks available to them would not have an inflationary effect on the local economy. While this solution might have been cumbersome, it was at least a realistic, commonsense approach.

Unfortunately, the proposal evoked only the habitual responses from the War Department. Major General John J. Hilldring, chief of the civil affairs division of the War Department special staff, commented that Congressional action would be required to institute such a procedure. The War Department usually seemed loath to approach Congress with its fiscal problems and considered Congressional action tantamount to the impossible. However, if it had foreseen Congress' interest in currency control after the Army's failure in this area resulted in a national scandal, it might have been slightly more willing to request legislation. A further response to Colonel Bernstein's suggestion came from General Hilldring and General Richards. They thought any withholding of pay "would be contrary to the ingrained rule that a soldier's pay is inviolate and that he can spend it as he considers best." [17]

Such unwillingness to revise ideas was fundamental to the cur-

rency control problem. General George S. Patton would not have
written a new chapter in the history of armored warfare if he had
been content to employ World War I tank tactics. Similarly, by
sticking to ingrained rules and not adapting currency control procedures to new situations, the War Department prevented this
administrative function from keeping pace with tactical innovations.
Another attitude which disabled effective currency control was
that servicemen had a right to convert gambling profits into dollar
credits. At the time that the War Department was protesting the
European theater's prohibition against reichsmarks, it had considered declaring gambling profits an illegitimate source of income.
Since unit commanders could certify only funds from official
sources for transmission to the United States, such a declaration
would cut down greatly on the quantity of money being transmitted
from Europe. Colonel Bernstein reported, however, that troop
commanders were very casual in their certification of funds for
transmission. Anyone could claim his money was from the gaming
table and get it certified. No effective method existed for determining what money was genuine gambling profits and what was directly
from the black market. Funds one soldier had looted, received
from civilians in exchange for commodities, or procured from the
Russians could be certified just as easily as those another soldier
had acquired from a bona fide crap game.

As long as the War Department allowed commanding officers to
certify gaming profits for transmission, no effective control could
be maintained. When the budget division of the War Department
considered outlawing gambling profits, it circulated its proposal
among other interested divisions. The Office of the Fiscal Director
and War Department G-1 approved the proscription of gambling
proceeds, but the civil affairs division of the War Department did
not. This "upholding by various individuals in the War Department
of the right of the soldier to transfer money he had won by games
of chance" was described by a representative of the budget division
as "the one factor which has always prevented an adequate control
of black market dealings in currency and of illegitimately acquired
currency." The budget division recognized these illegitimate transfers as a direct charge on War Department appropriations. The
Treasury Department concurred that a limitation on transmissions
to funds obtained from pay and allowances was imperative.[18] Each

day the Army postponed a decision on this basic question, the government was losing money.

An investigation made by the New York Finance Office, United States Army soon after the war substantiated the budget division's fears that currency control could never be successful so long as gambling profits, whether real or fictitious, were accepted for conversion into dollar credits. The New York Finance Office handled personal transfer accounts coming from overseas theaters into the United States. When it inspected all personal transfer accounts over $1,000, it found the justification invariably given was that the money represented gambling profits. The largest single personal transfer account transmission received up to December, 1945, was for $23,000.[19]

As the conflicting opinions among the staffs of the supreme headquarters, the European theater, the War Department budget division, the Washington Office of the Fiscal Director, and the War Department special staff concerning the Army's approach to currency control indicate, a lack of centralized responsibility was the chief deterrent to an effective currency control program. The old adage of too many cooks was forcefully documented by this episode. No agreement existed among divisions of the War Department as to what policy should be followed, and similar disagreement occurred among elements of the European theater. The War Department, despite its own indecision, wanted to monitor all phases of the theater's currency control program. Given the refusal of certain elements of the War Department and the European theater to sanction any genuine currency controls, it is little wonder that no effective policy was enacted before hostilities ceased.

The logical individual to have formulated and administered the European theater's currency control program was its fiscal director, General Cobbs, but a series of events made his efforts in this direction ineffective. Before the invasion of France on June 6, 1944, the fiscal director had been at theater headquarters in London and was responsible for currency management planning for Continental operations. His efforts were concerned primarily with the disbursing and accounting aspects of finance operations to the unfortunate exclusion of any planning for currency control.[20] Had his preparations for Continental finance operations included currency control, it is probable that his thinking would have been more influential when the need for stringent controls became dramatized.

By the time the currency situation grew serious on the Continent, the European theater fiscal director was no longer in a position to influence theater policy. On June 7, 1944, the theater's services of supply (the support echelon) was redesignated the communications zone, and the theater staff sections took command of the corresponding sections in the communications zone. The European theater fiscal director thus took charge of finance activities at both theater and communications zone headquarters. His functioning, however, became more aligned with the subordinate echelon. This identification with the inferior headquarters was the fiscal director's first step away from a position where he could have exerted influence in formulating currency control policy. His inability to carry his point on the April 19, 1945, prohibition of German indigenous currencies reflected his lack of status in theater councils. This was indeed unfortunate, since the fiscal director's desire to protect the interests of the United States government was the most realistic approach to currency control evidenced in the European theater.

General Cobbs was completely removed from the theater staff in July, 1945, when the communications zone was redesignated Theater Service Forces, European Theater (TSFET). The service forces staff emphasized that there was no longer an Office of the Fiscal Director at theater headquarters, which meant that the fiscal director had no active role in theater policy and that fiscal matters were considered unworthy of attention on the theater level. The removal of the fiscal director from an effective position accounts for the lack of serious attention given to his scrip proposal.[21]

When it became evident that the fiscal director was unable to inaugurate a workable currency control program, it was imperative that someone at theater headquarters assume responsibility for this function. The first to step into the breach was G-1 (the assistant chief of staff for personnel), who considered the problem in relation to troop morale and the social and political aspects of the black market. Although these considerations would temper any decisive action, G-1 was actually powerless to attack the real cause of trouble in occupied Germany: the decision of the four occupying powers—the United States, the Soviet Union, Britain, and France —to use identical Allied military marks. When Russia glutted the German economy with Allied military marks and American Army finance offices had to convert all types of marks into dollar credits, any attempt at currency control became futile.

| Chapter 4 | # Europe: The Debacle |

IF one factor could be singled out as the primary cause for the currency control debacle in postwar Europe, it was the Army's policy of exchanging all Allied military marks, regardless of their origin. Secondary to this policy was the Red Army's introduction of literally countless Allied military marks into the German economy. These two factors working together made Germany the most critical area for the Army's currency control program. Other European nations presented their peculiar difficulties and challenges, and this chapter will discuss currency control in its Continental dimensions, but the heart of the story, like that of the Continent, is Germany.

The initial difficulty was that the Allied powers agreed during hostilities on a uniform economic policy for occupied Germany. This meant that the same currency, Allied military marks, would be employed in all four zones. The Allies' putative objective was for the German economy to rebound as a unit so that Germany could resume its traditional place and responsibilities in European trade. They hoped that a refurbished German economy, in conjunction with a democratic government, would contribute to a restored equilibrium in Europe. Hindsight enables us to know that Russia never intended to pursue a quadripartite policy, economic or political, in occupied Germany. One of the first indications might have been her activities in regard to the Allied military marks.

As plans were being made for the German occupation currency, the United States assumed that the Soviet Union, as well as England and France, would be ethical in using Allied military marks. This false assumption concerning the Russians brought the American Army to grief. The Treasury began working on the design for the Allied marks in the first week of January, 1944,[1] and during the following month, the Russian government began its efforts to secure the plates used to print the currency. Dr. Harry Dexter White, Assistant to the Secretary of the Treasury, was the key figure in the Treasury's negotiations concerning the plates, and it was he who furnished the advice that Henry Morgenthau, Jr., Secretary of the Treasury, acted upon.

The stiffest resistance to the Soviet government's request for the plates came from A. W. Hall, director of the Bureau of Engraving and Printing. He objected to giving the Russians the plates because once the plates left the control of the American government, there could be no exact accounting for the amount of German occupation currency produced. To Hall any lack of specific responsibility in the production of currency was an anathema, a violation of the basic principles of his bureau.

General George C. Marshall, speaking for the Combined Chiefs of Staff in a letter to the Secretary of the Treasury, suggested that the printing plates be furnished the Russian government so long as the action did not interfere with General Eisenhower's currency needs. After the Secretary of the Treasury received General Marshall's comments, he conferred with James C. Dunn, Assistant Secretary of State, who informed him that the State Department desired to furnish the plates to the Soviet government if at all possible. Having received the concurrence of the Combined Chiefs of Staff and the Department of State, the Secretary of the Treasury decided on April 14, 1944, to give the Soviet government the printing plates for Allied military marks.[2]

This episode concerning the transmission of the printing plates to the Russians was one of the highlights in the posthumous furore that surrounded Harry Dexter White. Although never identified as a member of the Communist party, White was accused by Whittaker Chambers, former senior editor for *Time* and leading apostate from the American Communist party, of being a "willing and witting tool" of the Russian Communists. Before the war White wrote weekly or biweekly digests of the pertinent documents and information that came to his attention in the Treasury. One such summary in White's handwriting was found among Chambers' celebrated "pumpkin papers." [3] Elizabeth Bentley, a confessed Communist, testified before a Congressional committee that Soviet agents pressured White to secure for them a sample Allied military mark and that he complied. For some reason this specimen did not suit the Russians, and they then demanded the actual printing plates. Miss Bentley said that White dutifully went to work and acquired the plates for the Soviets.[4]

If White's actions regarding the printing plates were Communist-inspired, the official records of the War and Treasury departments do not suggest such inspiration. Given his proven predisposition toward the Russians, it would be safe to assume that if Soviet agents demanded this action of him, he would have endeavored to comply. Yet it would be well to maintain some critical reservation concerning the source of the allegations against White. He might have acted in this case without prodding from Soviet agents—or even without a thought of aiding the Communist conspiracy. It is safe to conclude, nevertheless, that White was the figure in the Treasury who masterminded the transfer of the printing plates and recommended a course of action to the Secretary of the Treasury. Whatever White's inspiration, his ideas were finally endorsed by men whose loyalty to the United States no reasonable person would ever question.

On April 18, 1944, the Bureau of Engraving and Printing delivered the plates, inks, and paper necessary for printing the German occupation currency to the Washington National Airport. There the material was loaded on five Russian airplanes which flew back to Moscow via Siberia.[5] When the American government gave the plates to the Soviets, it presumed they would print and put into circulation only the minimum currency needed in occupied Germany. The United States government could have had no idea the Russians would unloose a plethora of Allied military marks to flood the Germany economy.

Just thirteen months after the Treasury Department had given the plates to Russia, Germany became deluged with marks. When the Army first made contact with the Russians in May, 1945, it realized that the Russian command was distributing Allied military marks without measure. Russian finance officers were not accountable for the marks they disbursed, and they made payments without regard to troop pay scales in any quantities the soldiers requested. Often Russian soldiers were given Allied military marks by the handful with their rations. In spite of the barriers between the American and Soviet zones in Germany, United States forces began to receive large quantities of marks from German civilians, Russian soldiers, and displaced persons in exchange for cigarettes, candy, and soap. This trade in commodities became one of the distinguishing features in the economy of occupied Germany. On occasion Russian soldiers even made gifts of marks to their American counterparts. The supreme headquarters warned the War Department on May 24, 1945, that this behavior of the Russians was endangering the Army's entire monetary program.[6]

At the time General Eisenhower, supreme headquarters commander, sent his warning to the War Department, finance men had not seen enough Russian-printed marks to be able to identify them easily. On the basis of the marks that had come into American hands by May 24, General Eisenhower notified Washington that the distinguishing characteristics of the Russian marks were the paper and ink used in printing and a dash before the serial number. It was soon established that all Russian-printed Allied military marks could be identified by the dash.[7] This should have been the time for the War Department, or the Treasury, or the theater commander to have forbidden all further usage of Russian-issued marks in official channels of the United States Army. Although the supreme headquarters warned that the Army's entire monetary program was endangered, no party acted decisively. The implications of the obvious facts seemed not to have registered strongly enough on anyone in a position of authority. The Russians were distributing millions of identifiable marks, while the American Army continued with its established policy of converting military currencies into dollar credits. General Eisenhower foresaw that these Allied military marks issued by Russia could easily be converted into dollar credits through the Army's finance offices, but no one took the responsibility for shutting off the Russian onslaught.

The Office of the Fiscal Director in Washington, rather than act-ing on General Eisenhower's warning, requested on May 28 that the European theater make a report at the earliest moment on the Russian Army's basis for distributing marks. It also wanted to know how many marks were getting into the hands of American soldiers. Four days after receiving the supreme headquarters report of May 24 warranting action the Office of the Fiscal Director asked for a further report that would have had to be in the nature of a staff study![8] It was unfortunate that those responsible for Army administration did not realize that decisive action sometimes was demanded of them just as it was of tactical commanders. The result of inaction in this particular case was an overdraft of approximately $217,000,000 in Allied military marks *alone*.[9]

Finance officers in the field were quick to realize the danger of Russian-printed marks to the Army's appropriations. The Army was not supposed to collect any more money than it had disbursed as pay and allowances, and any collections in excess of this amount would result in a deficit. The finance officers knew that if they made wholesale conversions of Russian-printed marks an overdraft was inevitable. As long as they were supplied with American-printed Allied military marks, many disbursing officers refused to accept the Russian-printed marks from soldiers.

In pathetic contrast to finance officers' awareness of the situation was the report of a military government officer. He failed to see how a combination of scarce items from post exchanges and a superabundance of Allied military marks could produce inflated prices. His comments of May 30, 1945, were extremely naive and so indicative of a fundamental defect in the Army's currency control policy that they must be quoted extensively:

Troop spending will be in Allied Military Marks, but it is not now and is not expected to be for some time a factor of much significance in the German economy. The present shortage and rationing of civilian supplies, plus the non-fraternization rules, plus the increased better facilities offered by G.I. agencies all tend to reduce troop spending in civilian markets to a minimum and to give Allied Military Marks a separate circulation of their own without relation to and without significant influence on the German economy. Such trading as there is with civilians is likely to use post exchange rations as the main medium of exchange—which certainly is not an inflation of currency. . . . Reports of the inflationary influence from Russian use of Allied Military Marks appear to be distorted and exaggerated and to ignore the other factors. . . .[10]

In July, 1945, the finance officer of the Berlin district ordered all Russian notes segregated as they were collected and specified that no disbursements be made with them. But he was told by the theater fiscal director that they should be considered the same as American-issued marks. After this pronouncement was made, the Berlin district collected and disbursed the Russian marks freely.[11] Colonel George R. Gretser, finance officer for the Twenty-second Corps, foresaw the difficulty with Russian-printed marks and wrote a series of protests to the theater fiscal director. European theater headquarters replied that its policy was to accept Russian-printed marks on a par with those printed in the United States. Despite this policy, Colonel Gretser directed his five disbursing officers to accept no Russian marks. He maintained this injunction until his subordinate officers were supplied with Russian-issued marks. After that, resistance was futile.[12]

Given a combination of the above factors it was inevitable that Berlin, where soldiers of the two nations first came together in large numbers, would become the regnant city of the black market. The story of the operations of a single soldier—"Joe" for convenience —on the Berlin black market illustrates why the situation there was critical and reveals the laxity throughout the Army's system of currency control. The story is a true one.

Joe was with the first American unit to move into Berlin, the Second Armored Division. When he arrived there on July 4, 1945, he found that the Russians had already stripped the city. Some Russian soldiers told Joe they had not been paid for six months, but that when they reached the German capital they were given as many marks as they wanted. This currency was worthless to them except in Berlin since no provision existed for converting it into ruble credits in Russia.[13] In this respect, the Russians were using Allied military marks in the same way the *Wehrmacht* used its occupation currency, the *Reichskreditkassenscheine*.

The first things GI's started selling to the Russians were watches. A starting price for an American watch was 5,000 Allied military marks, or $500; some Swiss watches would bring from $1,000 to $1,200. Joe kept the $500 he made from the sale of his watch and used it to go into a partnership with a friend who was flying to Seventh Army headquarters. The flyer bought more watches in post exchanges and took them back to Berlin. During the two weeks he was in Berlin, Joe netted $50,000 from the sale of 100 watches! Getting 500,000 marks converted into dollar credits was just as much of a challenge as their acquisition. Joe's methods for this conversion were as resourceful as for his sales. First, in one day Joe put an amount equal to his total earnings in the Army into soldier's deposits. Then on returning to Paris, he invested in art objects and mailed them to the States.

After leaving the French metropolis, Joe went to Camp Lucky Strike, one of the many redeployment depots named after American cigarettes. There he exchanged his marks for francs with other soldiers. Those preparing for shipment back to the United States had already had their money converted into dollars. From these, Joe bought twenty-dollar bills for 500 marks each. The sellers could then return to a finance office and reconvert their newly acquired marks. Of course, there were risks involved for those making multiple conversions, but few speculators engaged in the money market without some thought of risk. With the francs he received in other exchanges, Joe also bought twenty-dollar bills from Frenchmen.

By the time Joe got on the transport, he still had an ample number of marks left. Once on shipboard many servicemen thought their foreign currency would be worthless, since they had been told conversions would not be made in the United States. Joe did not know what would await him when he got home, but he hung onto his money and hoped his fortune would hold. The first thing he saw when he arrived at the finance office at Camp Miles Standish, Massachusetts, was this sign: "ANY KIND OF FOREIGN CURRENCY EXCHANGED HERE." Joe took a reasonable portion of his remaining marks to be exchanged and farmed the excess out among buddies, retaining a percentage of their dollar redemptions. These were the final steps in the conversion of 500,000 Berlin black-market marks into American dollars.

This story of Joe multiplied scores of times was the reason that July, 1945, was a lush period for the Berlin black market. In that month American soldiers in the Berlin sector drew $1,000,000 in pay, yet managed to transmit $3,000,000 to the United States.[14] Despite the fact that no measures had been taken by the end of July to regulate this situation, the War Department representative to the European theater, Colonel Carl H. Pforzheimer, Jr., felt that it would gradually rectify itself as the Russians used up their liquid funds and as American soldiers ran out of things they wanted to sell.[15]

On August 3, 1945, when currency controls were being weakened throughout the theater, Colonel Pforzheimer stated his philosophy of control: ". . . the approach to currency problems should be made, not on a narrow military regulation basis, but rather from the governmental point of view. That is, the Army should at this time approach currency control as it affects the currency in use in zones for which it is politically, economically, and financially responsible, from an overall point of view and not merely as a problem in trying to establish safeguards against the ingenuity of a relatively small number of military personnel." [16] The overdraft in Germany of $271,000,000 proved either the *extraordinary* ingenuity of a relatively small number of soldiers or Colonel Pforzheimer's fundamental lack of understanding of the difficulties that faced the Army in occupied territories.

The Berlin district reported that during the period May 8 to September 30, 1945, a sum equaling six or seven times the amount of troop pay had been transmitted out of the city. The money had been derived from the sale of personal property. On August 9 an attempt at restriction was made. A limit equal to the sum of pay and allowances, plus 10 per cent (the inevitable allowance for gambling profits) was put on the amount which could be transmitted out of the theater in any one month. The Berlin district specifically stated for the first time that funds offered for transmission had to be derived from pay and allowances. In addition the Berlin district directed all persons, excepting officers of field grades and above, to submit applications for transmittals of funds to their commanding officers. Commanding officers had to certify that they had inspected the sources of funds being offered for transmittal and had found them legitimate. Field grade officers and above made their own certifications.[17] The effect of these restrictions was immediate: only half as much money left Berlin during the last three weeks of August as had been transmitted during the first week alone.[18]

Without a doubt one of the cleverest methods of removing profits from Berlin was the guise of cabling flowers to the United States. The Mackay Radio Corporation instituted such a service, and the flow of money to the States swelled. Soldiers would cable large sums to hometown florists ostensibly for flowers to be delivered to their families. The florists, rather than delivering flowers, would take money instead. Naturally, for the use of their services, the florists withheld a certain percentage from each transaction. Much black-market money cleared Germany through this channel before it was discovered and banned in November, 1945.[19]

After a time the black market in Berlin began to simmer down. When closer restrictions were put on the mails, servicemen were deprived of a good source of receiving from home the desiderata of the German economy. Furthermore, after a few months they exhausted the supply of watches and cameras they had used in trading with Russians. They then turned to selling their post exchange rations, for most consumer commodities were in short supply on the war-ravaged German economy. Cigarettes became a standard medium of exchange in the Berlin black market, as elsewhere in Germany. With cigarettes a soldier could command some of the choicest items on the German markets—sterling silver, china, porcelain, and jewelry. From time to time various rumors were circulated with the intent of curbing the black market, and a frequent one was that the Criminal Investigation Detachment was going to crack down. These threats managed to frighten away the timid, but even investigations did not deter the hardy.

As the occupation became more settled, soldiers were less interested in immediate profits than in long-range comforts. Goods that had been used in the black market became the means for attaining personal pleasure.

Since currency control violations in Berlin were flagrant from the viewpoint of the American Army, it would be well to consider the general state of the German economy during the initial stage of occupation. The war was responsible for the loss of over one-third of Germany's national wealth. Transportation was largely disrupted; industrial and agricultural production was only one-third of the prewar levels, and the money supply was inflated 600 per cent.[20] Yet, in the face of such bleak statistics, the German economy was comparatively well regulated. One economist has concluded without qualification that "in the first year of occupation the volume of cash transactions did not amount to much." [21] Another stated that in the first three years of occupation, price controls were "surprisingly effective." Most goods sold at legal prices, and wages and professional fees remained at prescribed levels.[22]

If the German economy was unusually well regulated during

those trying times, to what could the stability be attributed? Perhaps the safest answer is that the economic discipline imposed upon the German nation during the dozen years of the Nazi regime was not quickly dissipated. The German people were accustomed to a tightly controlled economy, and even the shock of defeat did not change their ingrained behavior markedly. This German penchant for following established routines is borne out by a story reported from Frankfurt during the final days of the war. In the midst of an American bombing raid on the city, as the walls of Hitler's Third Reich were literally crumbling down about them, faithful Frankfurt office workers, dressed in their usual business clothes, boarded their streetcars and rode dutifully to work.

That the full impact of Germany's war-torn economy was reflected in the Army's fiscal problems does not mean that the Army, alone, suffered, for virtually every phase of German economic life was tinctured to some extent by the black market's influence. This influence was appreciable, even if the black market accounted merely for what an economist described as "probably less than 10 per cent" of the total trading transactions.[23] Within this domain occurred some 90 per cent of the dealings in luxury items such as cameras, china, gems, silver, furniture, and rugs. Although it would be impossible to determine what percentage of transactions in staple items occurred in the black market, there existed a definable scale of prices for necessities. In the spring of 1947 black-market quotations in the American zone were approximately one hundred times the legal prices for soap, butter, sugar, saccharine, coffee, flour, hosiery, and flints. (Presumably prices were even higher earlier in the occupation.) Oleomargarine, liquor, and eggs commanded prices seventy-five times higher than the legal ceilings; whereas potatoes, beef, and Leica cameras sold for fifty times more than the legal limit. Coal, gasoline, rubber tires, light bulbs, suits, and dresses sold for prices twenty-five times higher than those prescribed governmentally, while electric wiring and typewriters sold at ten times the legal rate. Average black-market prices ranged between fifty and seventy-five times the legal prices.

Even though the German black market comprised something less than 10 per cent of the total transactions during the early occupation, it involved a great deal of currency, because of the extent of inflation. The volume of money in the black market was approxi-

mately 500 per cent greater than that circulating in legal transactions. Understandably, then, the black market siphoned off most
of the surplus currency in occupied Germany.[24] As a result the
postwar German economy was only *comparatively* stable. The sheer
volume of the black market presented acute problems to the oc-
cupier and occupied alike.

With the various interested agencies of the Army being unable
to devise a consistent currency control policy for postwar Europe
and with the German situation presenting unmistakable challenges,
it was natural that some level of command would feel sufficient
concern and responsibility to step in and do what it could to achieve
a semblance of order. Toward the end of hostilities, the European
theater's assistant chief of staff for personnel, G-1, had assumed
responsibility for currency control, but had done little about it.
The theater allowed the situation to continue through the summer,
but by autumn public opinion in America, as expressed in the
press, demanded action. The primary deterrent to any effective
action on G-1's part was the unsympathetic attitude toward currency control on the part of the theater commander, General Dwight
D. Eisenhower.

In August Colonel Pforzheimer had reported that General Eisenhower believed "all controls of foreign exchange transactions by
personnel under his command should be stiffened." [25] The following month saw a change in the General's thinking. He took a stand
against any restrictive measures aimed solely at his theater, for he
did not want his men to suffer in comparison with those in other
theaters because of currency arrangements concluded at the national level. That Europe was the area with the greatest need for
currency control apparently did not influence the commander's
opinion.[26] His ideas were shared, quite logically, by his chief of
staff, Lieutenant General Walter Bedell Smith. Although General
Smith was "fully aware of the effect of unlimited mark conversions
upon the United States taxpayer, as well as of the secondary effect
upon our financial relations with net troop pay countries," he
nevertheless wanted no currency controls tailored especially for the
European theater.[27]

Reflecting the European theater commander's philosophy of currency control was a foreign exchange control card proposed by the
theater to the War Department. After an individual had declared his

assets, both in cash and in the bank, and had *justified* any excessive amounts (the wording here is important for it demonstrates the theater's desire to keep the troops happy rather than to control transmissions), his declaration was to be entered on a card. Before the cards became the controlling instruments for transmissions to the States, individuals were allowed to send home their current assets. Thereafter, a soldier could transmit out of the theater one month's unencumbered pay (money actually drawn at the pay table), plus 50 per cent during any single month. This 50 per cent differential certainly belied any real desire to restrict transmissions to pay and allowances. The European theater informed the Department that before such a system were adopted, its provisions should be applicable to all overseas theaters. Furthermore, it suggested that any deficit the Treasury might develop could be charged to Germany and Japan as occupation costs.[28]

This foreign exchange control card of the European theater never was put into effect; rather, G-1 devised a directive limiting funds that could be transmitted out of the theater during any thirty days to one month's unencumbered pay, plus 10 per cent. This directive of September 28, 1945, specified that funds offered for transmission had to come from official sources. G-1 placed the responsibility for determining and certifying the source of funds on troop commanders. Unfortunately, this action of G-1 was misguided. Initially, G-1 approached currency control from the wrong angle—the September 28 directive tried to control the black market, not the currency. With the existing conditions, it was erroneous to assume the United States Army could control the European economy. The only thing it could have aspired to regulate was its own transmission of money back to the States. But G-1 predicated his entire policy of currency control on a regulation of the source of money offered for exchange and not on a strict control of what was accepted. When the need was for specific, ironclad rules, G-1 spoke of the necessity for money coming from official sources. Instead of stating that a sergeant may send home *only* $75 a month, G-1 said, "The appropriate commander . . . is charged with assuring himself that the funds sought to be transmitted by the applicants concerned were derived only from United States official sources." [29]

A second serious mistake arising from the directive was the failure to place actual control in the hands of the transmission agencies, such as finance offices and Army post offices. On the contrary, not realizing that unit administration was too attenuated in situations of wide troop dispersal to regulate individual currency speculation, G-1 depended on unit commanders to determine the source of funds. A further miscalculation concerned the interest of unit commanders in regulating the transmission of their men's funds. Colonel Bernstein, chief of the supreme headquarters G-5 currency section, reported that unit commanders were very casual in authorizing transfers of funds.[30] Finally, there was a demoralizing aspect in this directive since G-1 allowed only majors and higher ranks to certify the source of the funds they presented for transmission. All others had to be checked by their unit commanders.

The result of these miscalculations was a "costly and haphazard administration which engendered an atmosphere of subterfuge, resentment, and suspicion among the various levels of personnel." [31] The system in effect penalized the honest by complicating the transmission of actual pay and allowances. Even as this system was introduced, the European theater was undermining it by warning men to get excess funds out of the theater before the introduction of currency control books on November 1, 1945.[32]

As if the September 28 directive were not sufficiently innocuous, General Eisenhower decided by October 2 that this temporary stopgap was "unnecessarily restrictive." He intended to modify it quickly unless he received contrary instructions from the War Department.[33] Washington, however, approved the measure until something more substantial could be introduced.[34] In fact, rather than concurring with the General, the Department announced to the commanders of the other theaters that it was "seriously disturbed over the illegal acquisition of local currency by troops, particularly in Germany, Holland, Belgium, and France. . . ." [35]

Another deterrent to the institution of any effective currency controls in the European theater by early autumn was the attitude of the theater's fiscal director. He contended that currency controls were "impracticable and not feasible of implementation" while troops were redeploying en masse. Before the theater fiscal director made this pronouncement in Washington, the Army Service Forces Office of the Fiscal Director had been trying to devise a foreign exchange control system. After his visit, the Washington office virtually ceased its efforts along these lines.[36]

Although G-1 had made some effort at currency control in the European theater, his attempts were unappreciated by most echelons. The theater commander and chief of staff were basically opposed to restrictive measures, and troop commanders considered them an unnecessary administrative nuisance. The lack of cooperation G-1 received from field commanders in enforcing various directives, while evidence of their impracticality, also gave an insight into the command psychology. The Ninth Army, with the approval of the Twelfth Army Group, in April, 1945, actually recommended removal of controls, pleading too great an administrative interference with the savings program.[37] Several commanding generals overtly authorized their officers and men to disregard G-1's attempts at currency control.[38]

The basis of this behavior is understandable if one considers the attitude that high-ranking officers would develop after carrying men through the heat of battle into victory. They would be partial to their own men and try to protect their special interests against any administrative interdictions from the outside. The regard some generals had for their men led them to be indulgent and consider any troop misbehavior in the black market or the boudoir merely a frolic—a manifestation of the vital spirit that led to victory on the firing line.

While Germany held the center of the black-market stage, other European countries also offered the Army currency control troubles in the occupation period. Basic to these problems were the decrease in productive capacity resulting from wartime devastation and the concomitant scarcity of consumer goods. Coupled with such a situation usually was a great increase in the monetary supply. The impact of the war on Italy's economy is reflected in the following statistics. Wartime destruction was estimated to equal one and one-half to two years' national income, and the real national income in 1945 was approximately one-half that of 1938 (the prewar norm). In 1945 agricultural production was 58 per cent of that of 1938, and industrial output was 23 per cent of the 1938 figure. Accompanying these diminutions was a twelvefold currency inflation between 1940 and May, 1945.[39]

Citizens of Italy, possessing currency but few goods, were only too willing to pay inflated prices in the black market for necessities.

And there were always some American soldiers ready to sell post exchange items for a premium, hoping to convert some of their profits into dollar credits in the United States. But because of the small number of troops in the Mediterranean theater in the postwar period, currency control violations there were comparatively minor. Furthermore, the theater had consistently maintained throughout the war an aggressive program of currency control.

In Italy most exchange violations involved postal money orders as a means of transmitting illicit funds to the United States. Unit censorship on transmission of funds ended in the Mediterranean theater on V-E Day, and one private stationed in Naples took the end of censorship as a signal to get all his black-market profits out of the theater. When an Army post office alerted the provost marshal, he arrested the soldier. At the time of his arrest, he had $200 in blue seal dollars and $2,800 in money orders. The private claimed to have sent $5,000 in money orders to his wife in Brooklyn in the ten-day period after V-E Day.[40]

The frequent misuse of postal money orders in Italy prompted the United States Post Office Department to hold an inspection. The investigation revealed that many American soldiers were cooperating with Italian civilians in the money order racket. Italians would meet servicemen in bars, hotels, and other gathering places and offer to pay them as much as a 45 per cent bonus on the value of money orders purchased. Soldiers would take the lire from the Italians and buy money orders at the nearest Army post office, usually employing fictitious names for the remitter and payee. Then they would endorse the money orders and turn them over to the contact man, who would pay soldiers their commissions. One of the servicemen involved in the scheme was told by a liaison man that the lire used to finance the illegal transactions came from Vatican City. The postal inspector had not definitely determined how the Italians sent the money orders to the United States for payment, but he suspected that exchange facilities in the neutral enclave were used.[41] This was a logical suspicion, for Vatican City proved during the war to have unique advantages, because of its special status, as a center for black-market currency exchange.[42]

In Italy American soldiers were paid in lire at the request of the Italian government, but in some areas, such as the Balkans, it was impractical to use any currency other than dollars. Of course, the use of any American currency in Europe was risky because of inflationary conditions, and only because so few troops were involved could the American government afford to use yellow seal currency in the Balkans. The introduction of any large volume of American dollars might well have disrupted any Balkan economy, but the American government believed that it would cost less to use yellow seal dollars than to establish exchange machinery for each nation. Neither the United States nor any Balkan government was happy about the use of yellow seal dollars, but it seemed to be the most expedient measure. Although individual American soldiers sometimes were discriminated against by local money changers, they more often benefited because of the greater purchasing power of the American dollar on inflated economies. Individual Balkan citizens who possessed American dollars also profited, but their governments got no compensation for net troop pay.[43]

Runaway inflation in the Balkans immediately after the war sometimes worked against the interests of individual American servicemen. When soldiers dealt individually with local money merchants, who would trade dollars for local currencies at rates extremely unfair to the soldier, they were apt not to get the full value of their dollars.[44] As an expedient, American soldiers in Rumania pooled their dollars and bargained collectively for Rumanian currency.

Black-market activities in France were never as flamboyant as in Germany, but they were constant. The unrealistic rate of exchange of 50 francs to the dollar encouraged troops to enter the black market when they first landed in France. As the war and occupation progressed, inflationary conditions made the 50-to-1 rate even less tenable. During the last months of the war and into the postwar period, France experienced a steady price and currency inflation. Between January and March, 1945, the raw materials price index rose 43 per cent, but from March to December, only 25 per cent. From January to July, 1946, the wholesale price index rose something less than 20 per cent. Accompanying these increases in prices (and to some extent responsible therefor) was the rise in the number of francs in circulation. The amount of currency extant in

December, 1945, was 356 billion; in June, 1946, 438 billion; and in December, 1946, 492 billion.[45]

Basic to the economic grievance of the American soldier in France was the artificial pegging of the franc at the 50-to-1 rate. If soldiers were going to realize any purchasing power from their pay, they had to buy post exchange items and then peddle them on the black market.[46] Since servicemen got involved in unlawful dealings by trying to "get their money's worth," it would seem logical that the American Army would be liable to censure. The Army, however, offered a strong case in its own defense. Colonel Pforzheimer contended that the French government was primarily responsible in that it overvalued its franc. Had the exchange rate been realistic, soldiers would probably not have dealt so extensively in the black market.[47] Robert P. Patterson, Under Secretary of War, thought that any blame devolving on the American government because of troop participation in the French black market should rest on the shoulders of the State and Treasury departments, since they, and not the War Department, had accepted the 50-to-1 rate. Patterson was eager to write the offenders asking for prompt relief.[48] His partisanship might be considered admirable, but his facts in this particular case were wrong. The 50-to-1 rate of exchange was determined at the Casablanca Conference by President Roosevelt, Prime Minister Churchill, and the French provisional government.[49]

The French government had ambivalent desires concerning the relation of the franc to the dollar. On the one hand, it wanted to maintain the 50-to-1 rate because of the prestige it gave the franc, and on the other, it wanted to devalue the franc in order to derive more revenue in the form of net troop pay. The net troop pay agreement of August 25, 1944, stipulated that the American government would reimburse the French for the francs it drew from the French government to pay servicemen. When finance officers had ample francs, however, the Army would have no cause to request francs from the French. Such amplitude came from conversions of black-market profits into dollar credits.

If soldiers sold commodities, especially cigarettes, soap, and candy, on the black market, they usually converted their franc proceeds into dollar credits in finance offices. These conversions were in violation of exchange regulations, but as long as troop commanders were certifying the legitimacy of their men's funds, there was little choice but to make the conversions. Finance officers, having more francs than they had anticipated, naturally did not requisition more francs from the French government for pay purposes; they disbursed the francs coming from the black market. In this way, French black-market dealers were getting the benefit of post exchange commodities, but the French government was deriving no benefit at all in the form of net troop pay.

The disparity between the official and free-market value of the franc became so great by the summer of 1945 that the French government decided to take some remedial action. Although unwilling to forego the 50-to-1 rate of exchange for general transactions, it made a special concession to the American Army in establishing a fund for adjusted franc payments. Without devaluing the franc, the French government provided for each American serviceman in France an extra 850 francs per month to compensate for the difference between the official and actual value of the franc. On August 25 the French government turned over to the Secretary of the Treasury 975,000,000 francs ($19,670,625), the initial three-month supply. These arrangements had been approved by President Harry S. Truman, General Eisenhower, and the War Department.[50]

The European theater adopted the following arrangements for making the adjusted franc payments. Beginning with the August 31 payday, each officer and enlisted man permanently stationed in France drew 850 additional francs, without regard to grade. Those coming into France on leave got the adjusted franc payment, as did those arriving on official orders. Officers and enlisted men spending more than eleven days of temporary duty in France were eligible for the payment. They could not get another 850 francs, however, until they had spent thirty days in the country. No adjusted franc payments could be made outside France.[51]

The French government finally was forced to acknowledge that the 50-to-1 rate was no longer tenable. No further patchwork of interim measures could sustain an exchange rate too patently unrealistic. Consequently, the French government devalued its franc on December 26, 1945. The new rate was 120-to-1. Quite possibly more currency exchanges resulted from this devaluation of the franc than from any other postwar devaluation in Europe. Not only was the French metropolitan franc devalued from $.020175 to $.00840625 but the west African franc as well. For the military purposes of accounting, collecting, disbursing, and transferring funds, the new official value of one franc was $.008406.[52]

The agreement between the United States and France protected quasi-official funds, such as those of service clubs, and American servicemen from loss by collecting francs at the old rate and exchanging them at the new. According to the 1945 agreement between the French and American governments, the only losses reflected were to be in official disbursing accounts. In all theaters losses were compiled by the fiscal director and the total figure presented to the French government. By terms of the agreement, the French reimbursed the American Treasury for the cumulative loss. The Sixth Corps finance office, which sustained a devaluation loss of $10,269.63, thought the short notice on the devaluation was beneficial, despite the resulting confusion, because it prevented any attempts at profiteering on the exchange. For twenty days after the change in rates, the corps finance office processed late claims for exchange; those making late claims were required to execute a sworn statement that they had a legitimate cause for not getting their francs converted promptly.[53]

Although the Sixth Corps finance section might have been able to prevent profiteering after the revaluation of the franc, there seems to have been little effort at systematic control in Paris— soldiers could go to a finance office and exchange their francs by signing any name, as no identification was required. Many soldiers took this opportunity to convert black-market profits into legitimate dollar credits.[54]

Perhaps the American government's willingness in World War II, not just to protect the financial position of its soldiers but even to give them the benefit of the doubt, reflected a changing sense of the relationship between the government and its citizens. The government exhibited benevolent paternalism, often to its own detriment. This protection of funds of individual soldiers was in contrast to the World War I policy. During and after World War I when American soldiers exchanged dollars for foreign money, they had to reconvert at the current rate of exchange, thereby sustaining any loss resulting from devaluation.[55]

An illustration of how individuals, rather than the government, suffered after World War I concerns the franc devaluation in the summer of 1919. Immediately after the end of World War I, the Army gave officers stationed in Germany the option of cashing their pay checks in marks or francs. Because of the instability of the mark, most officers chose to receive their pay in francs. During the time they were in France, many officers and enlisted men had opened bank accounts; therefore, most of their liquid assets were tied up in France. The uncertain value of the mark induced many Army members in Germany to speculate on its exchange value in relation to the franc. As a method of curbing this speculation, the Army severely restricted exchanges between marks and francs. A man could exchange marks for francs only if he were on orders to go to France, and the disbursing quartermaster refused to cash officers' personal checks on French banks.[56]

The combination of these restrictions and an accumulation of assets in French banks meant that those having either French money or money deposited in France were unable to maintain much control over their funds. When the franc was devalued in the summer of 1919, individuals with French money were powerless to escape the loss. They had to stand by and see the savings of months vanish. During World War II the officer in charge of civil affairs, American forces in Germany, felt that the lesson to be learned from World War I was that the American soldier should be paid in dollars regardless of his place of service. Thereby, any loss resulting from currency devaluations would be taken by the government and not by the individual.[57]

Two main factors combined to doom military currency control in Europe to failure. The Army lacked a consistent, realistic currency control policy before the occupation began, and, once involved in the economic problems of a ravaged continent, it was unable to develop a satisfactory program. Currency control in Europe was a debacle, but those responsible were human and made human mistakes. Even though the errors seemed elementary, we must remember that hindsight is 20-20. Perhaps no other denouement could have been expected from the European fighting.

Chapter 5

The Far East

THE complexion of the currency control problem in the Far East at the outset of the occupation was considerably different from that in Europe. Most of the European theater's difficulties in this area were outgrowths of inconsistent and misconceived wartime policies, which proved grossly inadequate to cope with the occupation situation. A further difficulty besetting the European theater was that political and diplomatic considerations regarding Allied governments compounded currency control problems.

In the Far East none of these factors existed. The Pacific command, when it moved in to occupy Japan, was presented with a *tabula rasa*. No other nation's military forces were occupying Japan, so American policy could be unilateral. The command was not fettered with any established currency control policies, although some might have thought this a hindrance. But the European theater's wartime experience did not contribute to a better understanding of the currency control challenges it faced in the occupation period. Hence, a lack of firsthand knowledge could not have handicapped the Pacific command when compared with the European. Even though the Pacific command had no experiences of its own from which to learn, it certainly should have profited from the sullied record of the European theater, especially since the Japanese occupation did not begin until after some three and one-half months of fantastic currency control violations in Europe. Unfortunately, the Pacific command capitalized on none of its advantages and virtually recapitulated the Army's unhappy experience in Europe.

At the beginning of the occupation, the Pacific command adopted a supplemental currency, type "B" military yen, for use on the main islands of Japan—Honshu, Hokkaido, Shikoku, and Kyushu. This currency had been prepared some months before V-J Day, and had, in fact, already been employed on Okinawa. The Army had procured this military yen currency because it had to be assured of an adequate supply of yen, since it had no way to determine accurately the amount of Imperial yen it would have at its disposal. Actually, the Army found an ample supply of Imperial yen when it arrived in Japan and was never faced with a currency shortage, as it had been in North Africa and Italy. With the introduction of military yen in Japan, the Army announced that it would circulate on an equal basis with Imperial yen and that the latter would be fully acceptable in official channels.[1]

The initial currency control problem involved exchanging the yen of redeploying troops for dollars. The normal amount of money that was supposed to be exchanged was one month's pay and allowances, and as a guideline, the command established $150 as the maximum amount to be exchanged for a returnee. The soldier who presented more than this amount in yen for exchange had to sign an affidavit that the money was derived from pay and allowances and not from the sale of property or illicit black-market currency manipulations. When the soldier satisfied the finance officer that his funds were legitimate, he could put his yen in excess of $150 into postal money orders, soldier's deposits, or personal transfer accounts. Finance officers put the yen into one of the foregoing forms of dollar credits when American currency was unavailable for exchange.[2]

Finance offices in Japan were also responsible for exchanging yen for repatriated American nationals who had been interned by the Japanese during the war. If exchanges were not made in Japan, these civilians had great difficulty converting their yen, since their status as "unauthorized personnel" precluded the Army from making the exchanges at West Coast ports. When civilians did begin arriving in the United States with yen, the War Department reminded the Pacific command that it was remiss in its duty. Likewise, when redeploying troops landed on the Pacific Coast with substantial amounts of yen, the Department issued emphatic instructions to the command that all yen exchanges were to be made in the Far East in the interests of currency control.[3] Since there was a strict prohibition against the circulation of dollars in the Japanese economy, occupying forces coming from the United States had their currency exchanged within seventy-two hours after their arrival. Had dollars been allowed to circulate in Japan, they would have further disrupted the inflated economy.[4]

The economic situation in postwar Japan was considerably worse than in Germany. Japan not only had sustained extensive damage from bombing, thereby reducing its productive capacity, but was unable even in peacetime to produce sufficient consumer goods. In the early occupation period, therefore, serious shortages existed. Illustrating the decline of productive capacity are figures from two basic industries. Steel production declined 23.5 per cent from 1941 to 1945, while coal output slumped 70.9 per cent.[5] Whereas in occupied Germany the black market accounted for something less than 10 per cent of economic transactions,[6] in Japan by December, 1945, the people depended on the black market for half their daily needs. A year later the situation was slightly better, for by this time the Japanese were relying on the black market for only 20 to 30 per cent of their staple foods. Prices for these items were eight to nine times higher than official ceiling prices, "with which the average citizen had no practical connection in his daily life." These official prices were five to ten times higher than before the war. Unfortunately for the Japanese, wage increases had not kept pace with prices.[7]

The cornerstone on which the Pacific command built its currency control program for Japan, Korea, and Okinawa was the certification by personnel officers of the legitimacy of funds presented for conversion into dollar credits. With Imperial yen circulating in the military establishment on an equal footing with type B yen, the command thought this system of certification was necessary to prevent wholesale amounts of black-market yen from being converted into dollar credits. Each time an enlisted man presented money for transmission to the United States, the personnel officer ascertained its source. If the officer was satisfied with the legitimacy of the funds, he had the enlisted man sign a statement about their origin and sent them to the finance office along with a certificate stating: "I certify that I have personally inquired into and examined the source of the funds herewith transmitted, deposited, or used for purchase of war bonds and postal money orders and have determined that these funds were legitimately obtained as payment of pay and allowances from a finance officer of the United States Army and were not obtained from sale of property, black market currency operations, or other illicit sources." If a personnel officer had several transactions, he could group them on a single letter of transmittal to the finance office, including the name of each man and the amount of his transaction. When personnel and commanding officers felt incapable of determining the legitimacy of funds presented for transmission, they could forward all the data to the next higher echelon, which could decide on the proper action to take. Officers made their own certifications.[8]

The limitations of this system were recognized from the start. Colonel K. B. Rothnie, deputy fiscal director for the command, stated that the effectiveness of the system would depend on how thorough and conscientious personnel officers were in determining the source of funds presented for transmission. The command thought the personnel officer the logical individual to pass on the legitimacy of funds because of his close contact with the troops. Notwithstanding the fact that the success of the command's entire currency control program hinged on the reliability of the personnel officer, Colonel Rothnie thought this system was the way to prevent a repetition of the black-market traffic occurring in Europe.[9]

Even as the Pacific command announced its inadequate system of control, danger signs were appearing. On October 20, 1945, a United Press release from Tokyo revealed that a black market had sprung up in American food, cigarettes, and Army blankets. The story noted prophetically that when similar conditions prevailed in Europe, some American soldiers transmitted more money home in a week than they had received as pay in a year.[10]

Before the end of 1945, a full-blown Japanese black market had developed in American goods. This black market proved the downfall of the command's currency control program, since the laxity of the certificate system permitted soldiers to convert vast illicit profits into dollar credits. As in France, the involvement of soldiers in the black market was directly connected with the official rate of exchange between the dollar and yen. From the beginning of the occupation, the ratio of 15 yen to $1.00 established by the American government greatly overvalued the yen.

This overvaluation, according to the command's fiscal director, Colonel Harold S. Ruth, was "the largest single factor bringing about the conditions conducive to illegal operations. . . ."[11] Soldiers, by being paid in yen at the official rate of exchange, were deprived of the true purchasing power of the dollar. Their alternative was to enter the black market with goods from the post exchange and supply room. Soldiers could buy cigarettes, soap, and candy at reasonable prices in post exchanges, later selling these commodities at highly inflated prices on the black market. Since there was no property accountability, servicemen also sold their government-issue blankets, shoes, and clothing. These, too, commanded fancy prices on the black market. Personnel officers, through their inability or indifference in checking the source of yen presented for transmission, certified these tremendous black-market profits for conversion into dollar credits. The illicit proceeds so converted resulted in an overdraft of $74,000,000 in yen throughout the command.[12]

Another loophole, in addition to the certificate system, existed in the Pacific command's currency control system: the unregulated circulation of yen in the Army's retail outlets. A soldier could spend yen in post exchanges and quartermaster sales stores without any check being made on their source. This enabled the speculator to enter the black market on a revolving basis. He could buy commodities with the yen he drew as pay and sell them at inflated prices to the Japanese. With the proceeds, he could return to the retail stores and buy more goods. A saturation of the black market seemed to be the only limit to the profits an ingenious soldier could make in occupied Japan.[13]

Of the total overdraft in disbursing officers' accounts in the Far East, only about 20 per cent came in initially through finance offices. This percentage represented conversions of yen into war bonds, soldier's deposits, and personal transfer accounts. The remaining 80 per cent arrived in disbursing accounts via receipts from post exchanges, Army post offices, and quartermaster sales stores. These agencies exchanged their cash receipts for Treasury checks at finance offices. The fact that this great percentage came from commodity outlets, excepting Army post offices, is indication of soldier participation in the Japanese black market.[14]

The inability of the Pacific command to maintain currency control was not solely its own fault, according to Colonel Ruth. The limitations it placed on the reconversion of yen into dollar credits through the certificate system "could not be enforced to any degree of effectiveness under the control measures then prescribed by the War Department." [15] Whether the Department prevented the command from adopting more stringent measures to achieve currency control, as Colonel Ruth's statement might indicate, is problematical, for neither War Department nor the Pacific command records have revealed any such attempt. But the Department's attitude toward the European theater's currency control problems would lend credence to Colonel Ruth's statement.[16]

The currency control problems of the China theater after V-J Day were indeed slight when compared with those of the Pacific command. They were related directly to the procedures involved in phasing out a theater and indirectly to the continuing and aggravated matter of inflation. Immediately following the end of hostilities, a short break in the inflationary spiral occurred. Hoarded goods flooded the market, and gold prices fell throughout China— 90 per cent in Shanghai and 60 per cent in Chungking. In the latter Chinese National currency appreciated 100 per cent in relation to the United States dollar. A Chinese economist explains this reversal as resulting from an emotional release for the Chinese people after the privations of long years of war. However, this downward trend was short-lived. The resumption of the runaway inflation was partly due to the maladministration by the Chinese government of the conversion of the Japanese puppet-government currencies—notes of the Central Reserve Bank and Federal Reserve Bank. Exchange rates undervalued these currencies; consequently, price quotations in them were high. During the four-month conversion period, prices in Chinese National currency gradually rose to equal and then surpass those quoted for the puppet currencies.[17]

The greater the degree of inflation in China, the greater the temptation might have been to American servicemen to speculate in the money market. Illustrative of China's growing fiscal instability were the lessening amount of American dollar reserves behind its Chinese National currency and the tremendous accretion in the currency supply in the latter half of 1945. The Chinese government used, as part of its security for issuing Chinese National currency, its credit in the United States Treasury. This credit accrued partially from Chinese expenditures for the American Army during the war. Such expenditures were for construction, housing, and food furnished the Army by the Chinese government. In July, 1945, China's dollar reserves represented $1.00 (US) for every $538 (CNC) in circulation. By December, 1945, the ratio was $1.00 (US) to $1,200 (CNC). The last half of 1945 saw the volume of Chinese National currency expand from $462,327,000,000 in July to $1,031,900,000,000 in December.[18]

Since soldiers serving in China had been paid in dollars throughout the war, they were allowed to bring an unlimited amount of dollars back to the United States. Servicemen who traveled to the United States aboard a warship, troop transport, or military aircraft, were not questioned about the dollars they brought from China. If, on the other hand, they traveled by some other means and were carrying more than $500, they had to declare the entire amount. The declaration was only to satisfy Treasury requirements and in no way limited the amount that could be imported. Civilians returning from the China theater to the United States, however, could import only $50 in personal funds. They were instructed to convert any currency in excess of $50 into letters of credit, money orders, or traveler's checks.[19]

Even after V-J Day the China theater was still promoting the savings program as the most effective method of currency control. The theater stressed the beneficial effects of savings to a man returning to civilian life. It reported that with unemployment "becoming a factor in the United States," a man's savings could tide him over and keep him from having to accept the first job offered, "no matter how undesirable." This foreboding picture of America's return to a peacetime economy was combined with the consolation that no really good opportunities for spending existed in China. The theater recommended that its men avoid extensive purchases of souvenirs because of the tremendously inflated prices. Furthermore, money in the bank was "certain to serve a far more useful purpose than a locker full of trinkets." [20]

American forces in China were paid in dollars because of the hopelessly inflated economy; occupation forces in areas where there were few American troops, such as Formosa and the Balkans, were usually paid in dollars because the number of servicemen did not justify the establishment of exchange mechanisms. On Formosa American soldiers could exchange dollars for the foreign money if they wanted to make purchases locally, but they did so at their own risk, for there were no facilities for reconversion. This non-reconversion principle was a means of preventing black-market profits from being converted into dollar credits. Usually, the Chinese government funded American disbursing officers on Formosa with Chinese currency to be used for local purchases. When it was unable to do so, finance officers could use dollars as a temporary expedient. The Chinese government, however, wanted to keep the circulation of these dollars on Formosa at a minimum because of their inflationary attributes.[21]

Whereas the currency control problems in China and outlying islands were minor in the first year of the occupation, those in Japan were acute. The failure of currency control in Japan was tantamount to a failure throughout the Pacific command since the concentration of American troops in Japan was much denser than elsewhere in the Far East. Where the command might have profited by the well-publicized mistakes of the European theater, it demonstrably learned little. The maxim that those who do not know history are doomed to repeat it applied to the Pacific command in this respect. The Army's currency control experience in the Far East was a recapitulation of that in Europe.

Chapter 6	Currency Control Books

AFTER the Pacific command adopted its unwieldy certification system, it made little attempt to improve its currency control program until July, 1946, when it introduced type "A" yen.[1] The European theater, however, had made some systematic, though fruitless, efforts to maintain control over conversions before it resorted to scrip.[2]

The initial attempt of the European theater was in the form of a currency control book. Inspiration for this type of control did not originate in the theater but in the War Department. In the spring of 1945 the budget division of the War Department began considering exchange books as a method of achieving strict conversion controls. It recommended to the Office of the Fiscal Director that such a method be devised for introduction in the European theater. As of July 20 the Office of the Fiscal Director had produced nothing tangible but was involved in designing an exchange book which the individual soldier would carry with him as a permanent record of his fiscal transactions. General Richards, the War Department budget officer, thought that the books might be published before the end of the summer.[3]

When Colonel Pforzheimer, by this time the chief of the foreign financial branch of the budget division, studied the book devised by the Office of the Fiscal Director, he concluded that it was the answer to the currency control problem. He stated on August 3 that the book would provide "effective control, with the least number of loopholes, of conversion into dollars, in a manner that would not circumscribe such conversion by the G.I. up to the total amount of his pay. . . ." In other words, a soldier would be able to convert into dollar credits no more than he had drawn in pay, as reflected on his exchange book. This limitation, Colonel Pforzheimer thought, would obviate any further deficit. He believed that the use of books would require a 5 per cent staff increase in personnel offices, but that no material increase would be necessary in finance offices.[4]

After the Office of the Fiscal Director in Washington had devised an exchange book, the European theater fiscal director began working on a similar currency control book. G-1, who was responsible for currency control within the command, was eager to initiate the currency control books on September 15 and had requested War Department approval of the system.[5] On August 29, 1945, he outlined his proposal for the European theater chief of staff.[6] Inexplicably and revealing an amazing lack of coordination, on the same day, the European theater adjutant general announced to all subordinate echelons the theater's proposed adoption on November 1, 1945 of Circular 139. This circular explained in detail how the currency control books would be used. The adjutant general urged all personnel within the theater to prepare for the adoption of currency control books by converting "accumulated pay and allowances and other money derived from United States official sources in excess of current needs" into dollar credits during October.[7] Since unit officers had previously demonstrated their inability to restrict transmissions to money derived from official sources, it was certain they would not increase their efforts before a systematic attempt at currency control began. What the theater adjutant general's announcement amounted to, then, was an open invitation to convert all indigenous currency—pay, allowances, and black-market proceeds alike—into dollar credits during the month of October.

The implications of the directive were fully understood throughout the theater, but nowhere was it better appreciated than in Berlin. Servicemen in the German capital remembered well the fortunes that had been made in July, when $1,000,000 had been disbursed as pay and $3,000,000 had been collected through official channels. They were eager, in the best American tradition of competitive enterprise, to set a new record, and they did. The Berlin district disbursed as pay and allowances in October $2,570,921.32; yet it collected through finance offices, Army post offices, post exchanges, and quartermaster sales stores a total of $8,226,461.73! [8] Clearly, no one was trying to limit exchanges to funds derived from pay and allowances, plus the 10 per cent gambling differential.

When the American press heard of this unbelievable breakdown of currency control, it censured the Army sharply for a lack of stewardship with public monies. The New York *Herald-Tribune* pointed out that any conversion of funds into dollar credits in excess of those disbursed as pay and allowances resulted in an overdraft, which would probably mean a direct loss to the American tax-payer.[9] The New York *Times,* along with the *Herald-Tribune,* casti-gated the Army for not releasing the figures on disbursements and collections in the European theater.[10] The overseas service news-paper, *Stars and Stripes,* was fully as caustic as the New York press in its description of the Berlin bonanza.

Berlin, October 31. The Army's "Berlin Bank–Russian Division" otherwise known as the Berlin APO was awash with millions of dollars worth of money orders today as thrifty soldiers mindful of the Nov. 10 deadline when easy transmission of currency is expected to come to a drastic halt made a last minute rush to tuck their *savings* [italics mine] safely away.

Hundreds of soldiers stood in line through the night in order to slip their cash under the wire before the imposition of regulations that will tend to make it impossible to send home more than what could be accumulated from legitimate Army sources over a three-month period. The millions now pouring into the APO coffers here were derived from "official U. S. sources" of course, although most of the bills are marked with a hyphen before the serial number which is indicative of the money's Russian origin.[11]

The War Department was disturbed after it learned that the European theater was giving its men a month's grace before the introduction of currency control books. When statistical reports revealed the great volume of illicit funds being converted into dollar credits during October, the Department radioed a protest to the theater. It notified General Eisenhower that it intended asking him to send officers to Washington to justify "any unauthorized use of government funds which may result in a loss to the Treasury and force the War Department to seek an appropriation to cover such loss." [12] In reply, the theater headquarters explained that General Eisenhower personally decided to urge individuals to convert accumulated funds into dollar credits "because of large amounts of accumulated pay and allowances in possession of redeploying personnel which were being legitimately presented at Ports of Embarkation for exchange or transfer. . . ." [13]

Apparently by the time the theater made this reply on October 27, it had conveniently forgotten that on August 29 it had urged the command to convert accumulated funds because of the impending introduction of currency control books and not because of exchange difficulties at redeployment centers. Even if some redeploying troops were having difficulty converting funds into dollar credits, it is highly doubtful that General Eisenhower was justified in opening flood gates throughout the theater to facilitate exchange in one area. The deficit during October of almost $6,000,000 in the Berlin district alone would indicate the unsoundness of the commanding general's thinking.

Yet the theater refused the responsibility for operating a currency control program by stating that the real trouble lay in overvaluations of European currencies and "arrangements concluded at [the] national level. . . ." These factors, rather than any sanctioning of currency control evasions by the European theater, rendered "any stop gap measures of Army finance currency control inadequate and ineffectual." Furthermore, currency control measures were considered "unduly repressive" to the American citizen-soldier. The theater expressed certain reservations about its laxity resulting in an overdraft but suggested that "if in fact a deficiency in appropriation for the pay of the Army is the result of evasions of control measures," the overdraft "be set up as a reparation claim." [14]

As indicated above, Circular 139 had originally been scheduled to become effective on November 1, 1945, but the time was changed to November 10. On this date, currency control books were finally introduced in the European theater. The theater, even after extending the grace period, allowed a liberal initial declaration in the currency control book: a man could declare the total of his net cash pay for the three months prior to November 10, less any recorded transmissions to the States during that three-month period. Unit commanders certified the initial entries in their enlisted men's books. Commissioned officers and civilians certified their own declarations and maintained their own books, while personnel officers kept all other books. The currency control book provided columns for credit and debit entries, but the only necessary authentication for a transaction was the stamp or initials of the person handling the transaction. When a man was leaving the theater or making a permanent change of station, he would convert all indigenous currency and his book would be stamped "final payment." After that, no further exchanges could be made legally.[15].

The object of posting credit entries for pay and allowances and debits for funds sent home was to have a record of the currency any person might legally have in his possession. The theory was that with such a record it would be impossible to transmit out of the theater any money in excess of legitimate pay and allowances. The planners of the currency control book made a serious omission in not providing spaces for posting debits or reducing entries for personal expenses. The explanation G-1 gave for this crippling feature was that it would have made the system unwieldy and demoralizing.

A similar omission rendered the currency control books used by the First Cavalry Division in Japan ineffective. Members of this division, the only unit in the Far East experimenting with currency control books, did not have to enter in their books yen spent in post exchanges, quartermaster sales stores, or on telephone and telegraph messages to the States. This enabled them to transmit home all their pay and allowances and still live high on the Japanese black market.[16]

In the European theater, despite the fact that G-1 had assumed overall responsibility for currency control, the theater fiscal director was in charge of operating the currency control book system. One of the reasons he did not make formal recommendations to G-1 about including entries for personal expenses was that the format of the book was entirely inadequate to handle numerous debits.

Since the books were of the simplest format and construction and forging initials presented no obstacle to an "operator," the problems of counterfeit books and falsified entries should have been foreseen. Unprincipled and ingenious servicemen devised many methods to defeat the purpose of the books. Ordinary ink eradicator was frequently used to alter postings in the books, and the design provided space where extra figures could be added to recorded sums. A widespread loss of cards also enabled the losers to use their imaginations for new credit entries. Furthermore, it was not uncommon to find soldiers with three to four books, since they were not numbered serially.[17]

In many cases certifications by commanding officers were inaccurate. Frequently, unit commanders took a very casual attitude toward this administrative duty and certified funds without making any attempt to check their source. But even when troop commanders were conscientious about making certifications, they often encountered difficulties, principally caused by the frequent reassignment of units. As a result they had an inadequate knowledge of both the troops and the source of troop funds. Because of the pressure of time, they were unable to investigate fully and had to act on faith. Another reason for the ineffectiveness of the books was that they were not issued to everyone. Those entering leave centers and redeployment areas were allowed to transact their financial business without the restriction of books.[18] Dependents arriving in the theater were issued no currency control books, consequently their local currency exchanges were unregulated.[19]

Most finance and personnel officers directly responsible for the operation of this system realized immediately its weaknesses. The task of any officer having to verify the source of money presented for exchange was well-nigh impossible under the post-combat conditions. Major Delavan C. Clos, personnel officer for the Eleventh Traffic Regulation Group of the First Airborne Army, thought that it would be absurd to try to check the origin of the marks his men wanted to transmit to the States from Berlin. Realizing the aim of the currency control book, he established a card file for each man whose money he was supposed to check. On each card was the maximum amount a soldier could have drawn while overseas, and there would not be authorization for transmission of more than this amount. Usually finance officers in Berlin during this period were too busy to check personnel officers' figures; they had to assume the personnel officers knew their business. Consequently, the success of the system depended largely on the honesty and ability of the personnel officers.[20]

Colonel George R. Gretser, Twenty-second Corps finance officer in the occupation period, declared the currency control book a farce. The physical attributes of the books—their flimsiness and inadequate format—did much to defeat their purpose. "But even had these books been perfect," said Colonel Gretser, "they still would not have been the solution to the problem." They created an excess of administrative work and were too clumsy for the task. The need was not for a secondhand control, such as the books provided, but for a direct supervision of the currency in the men's hands. This type of control could be achieved only by using a United States currency. Since the blue seal dollar was forbidden in the European theater, a scrip currency was the solution. These opinions, according to Colonel Gretser, reflected the thinking of division disbursing officers: "They always seemed to have a keener insight into the real issues involved in currency control than those finance people at theater or War Department level who did the planning." [21]

After Circular 139 became effective in the European theater, no other overseas theater would exchange European currencies unless the individual requesting an exchange presented his currency control book. This restriction was to prevent illegal traffic in Continental currencies. If a person had never received his book, had lost it, or had departed the theater before the books were introduced, he could sign an affidavit to that effect and get his currency exchanged.[22] The Mediterranean theater adopted the currency control books on February 10, 1946, in an effort to prevent illicit currency traffic between the European theater and itself.[23]

The books prescribed by Circular 139 might have been some deterrent to the conversion of black-market profits into dollar credits, but they by no means solved the problem, as the following statistics demonstrate. In February, 1946, the officers and men of the European theater drew $25,218,344.16 in cash. They returned through official channels in that month $35,183,221.20.[24] The next month, they were paid $21,826,216 in cash; yet their March transmission of dollar credits to the United States was $36,482,480. Approximately $21,500,000 of the March transmission was returned through postal money orders.[25] Currency control remained a serious issue in the Berlin district during the first quarter of 1946. Figures consolidated from the books of the Fifty-sixth Finance Disbursing Section and the Seventy-eighth Division finance office show the net amount paid was $3,743,344.59, while cash collections at quartermaster sales stores, finance offices, post exchanges, and Army post offices came to $7,660,783.96.[26]

G-1 ascribed the failure of the currency control book program to the theater headquarters' lack of interest. It stated that the command had never taken "positive and vigorous measures to detect personnel engaged in black market activities." The breakdown of individual integrity in this area resulted in a general decline of both morality and morale. The morale of soldiers of principle suffered when they came in daily contact with men who boasted of their unlawful profits, and their respect for authority was likewise lessened when they saw men openly flouting currency control directives with impunity. G-1 considered continued unenforcement prejudicial to the good order and discipline of the Army.[27]

In the spring of 1946 an effort was made to correct this situation. On April 27 General Joseph T. McNarney, successor to General Eisenhower, ordered all troops in the Frankfurt area to stand reveille at seven o'clock. His order stated that the measure was taken in an effort to tighten discipline.[28] Obviously, the roots of the trouble in the European theater lay far too deep to be eradicated by making soldiers stand an early formation, but General McNarney's order was evidence that the command was not unaware that it faced an embarrassing situation.

Some observers believed the bad morale and discipline problems were caused primarily by black-market temptations. An "unwholesome atmosphere" was created in the European theater by the widespread impression that "engaging in some sort of racket [was] expected of occupation troops." A reporter from the New York *Times* cited some examples of how the sanctioning of illicit monetary transactions had permeated even those responsible for upholding and administering the Army's currency control program. A civilian employed by the information control division complained to an Army finance officer that he and his staff had not been paid for four months. The finance officer asked what difference it made, implying that anyone relying on his salary was passing up obvious opportunities. When the reporter cashed a money order at an Army post office in Frankfurt, the enlisted clerk at the window tried to involve him in a fraudulent entry in his currency control book. The chief of a military government detachment sent an enlisted man to Vienna monthly to peddle cigarettes, using the proceeds to buy porcelain, which he mailed home. Such violations clouded the Germans' view of American soldiers as ambassadors of democracy and caused them to consider the occupiers as, rather, mercenary and vulgar.[29]

After the books had been in operation for three months, G-1 admitted that Circular 139 had been a "shot in the dark." The many "bugs" in the system made G-1 realize that some corrective measures were mandatory. He did not want to attack the individual weaknesses piecemeal, realizing they were so manifold that the better course would be to wait and revise the system entirely.[30] As early as January, 1946, G-1 had begun to think in terms of an improved currency control book. On April 15 the European theater published Circular 50, which described what the new books would contain. The circular was to become effective one month later.

This second circular prescribed several improvements over the initial program. All servicemen and dependents authorized to use Army finance facilities were to retain their own books, which were numbered serially. Coupled with the improved design which provided space for reducing entries for personal expenses was the suggestion that agencies such as post exchanges, liquor stores, and Western Union sell coupon or chit books to reduce the debit listings.[31] The Berlin district inaugurated a chit book system in July, 1946. When an individual received a chit book from the finance office, he did not pay cash for it. The finance office merely deducted its value—$5, $10, or $20—from the balance in the currency control book. Each time a serviceman made a purchase at a snack bar, club, Army post office, quartermaster sales store, mess, or post exchange, he presented chits along with his money.[32] The labor required in accounting for chits made this system impractical. The Berlin district's experience was the basis for not incorporating chits in the final currency control book directive, Circular 82.[33]

Despite the improvements of Circular 50 over Circular 139, it never went into effect. The issuance of Circular 50 remains enigmatic, since as early as March, 1946, plans were being made to prevent its implementation. In that month the War Department first hinted at its interest in a scrip currency. Hoping that scrip would be introduced, the European theater fiscal director, Colonel Ralph A. Koch, was able to exert enough pressure on G-1 and other staff officers to scuttle Circular 50. Colonel Koch, successor to

General Cobbs, had always contended that chits would cause far more difficulties than they would eliminate. He thought that if a choice could be had between a secondary currency such as chits and a primary, substitutive currency such as scrip, the latter would be indubitably superior.[34]

In April when G-1 saw the February statistics on disbursements and collections, he realized currency control books were not the solution to the European theater's problem. Disbursements that month had been $25,218,344.16; $35,183,221.20 had been collected.[35] February was the first month since the introduction of the books that more funds were sent out of the theater than were disbursed. G-1 finally advocated a scrip currency as the only permanent solution to the dilemma.[36]

The War Department's serious consideration and implied approval of scrip had two direct consequences in the European theater: Circular 50 never was implemented, and G-1 prepared a final document revising currency control books. European theater Circular 82, June 3, 1946, became effective on June 20, but only as a decoy for the conversion to scrip. Although Circular 82 was intended primarily as camouflage, it provided for currency control books with several noteworthy improvements over those prescribed by Circular 139. These revisions were largely adaptations from Circular 50. The books were serially numbered and printed on substantial, watermarked paper. They were issued to each serviceman, rather than being maintained by personnel officers. All purchases of $5.00 made at official agencies were listed as debits in the new books, whereas earlier no reductions were made for personal expenses.[37]

Lieutenant General Joseph T. McNarney, commanding general of the theater, believed that although Circular 82 provided maximum regulation within the framework of currency control books, it was at best only a temporization. He stated that the "ultimately fatal weakness" of individual currency records was that no "satisfactory compromise could be reached between maximum academic effectiveness and maximum administrative feasibility. One quality can be improved only at the expense of the other, while neither can afford the sacrifice without material impairment of the objective sought." General McNarney wanted to make "unmistakably clear" to the War Department that the theater recognized the serious shortcomings of any form of currency control book and therefore urged the introduction of scrip "with the least delay." [38]

While recognizing the weaknesses of any kind of currency control book system, the European theater made a conscientious attempt to enforce Circular 82. In August, 1946, the theater headquarters, having been prompted by the War Department, instructed all echelons to conduct irregular, unannounced showdown inspections of currency control books. If an individual was found with more money in his possession than was recorded on his book, the surplus was confiscated. This stringent enforcement served a twofold purpose: it discouraged illicit currency dealings by demonstrating that the theater was finally serious about maintaining currency control, and it gave the impression that the system was a long-term operation and thereby served as a decoy for the conversion to scrip.[39]

| Chapter 7 | # Success With Scrip |

CONSIDERING the Army's failure to maintain currency control in either occupied Europe or the Far East, it is unfortunate that inspiration for the ultimate settlement of the problem did not have its genesis in the War Department. The Army's record would have appeared much better had it been able, finally, to resolve its own dilemma. Only at the insistence of the Treasury Department, however, did the Army begin to consider using a scrip currency.

On February 18, 1946, Fred M. Vinson, Secretary of the Treasury, proposed in a letter to the Secretary of War that overseas troops be paid in a combination of scrip and local currencies. Ignoring soldiers' legal entitlement to exchange pay into dollar credits, Secretary Vinson suggested that soldiers draw only enough local currency for immediate expenditures on the foreign economy and that there be no reconversion privilege. He described his proposal for scrip as a refinement of a suggestion made by the Treasury on October 17, 1945, that overseas forces be paid in military payment orders which they could cash for indigenous currencies but could not convert.[1] Secretary Vinson's letter attested the Treasury's annoyance with the War Department's apparent lack of concern with currency control:

For many months the Treasury Department . . . has been attempting with the greatest seriousness to induce the War Department to adopt measures which will prevent the conversion into dollars of foreign currencies acquired illegally or through unauthorized channels. These attempts by the Treasury Department have not met with success. . . . There has been no serious attempt by the War Department to investigate cases of Army personnel who acquired personal fortunes during the course of the military operations. . . . We are not even currently informed of the situation at any given time since the War Department has not or cannot obtain through its ordinary procedures significant statistics as to the amounts involved in its foreign exchange operations.

This situation is considered to be one of greatest gravity. The inability of the United States Army to prevent the conversion into dollars of foreign currencies acquired by personnel through unauthorized channels, and the unwillingness of the War Department to impose effective controls which the Treasury has in the past suggested, has resulted in a serious worsening of the situation and the Treasury now feels it necessary to propose a more drastic measure, which would render unnecessary and thus eliminate the Army's conversion system.[2]

This caustic rebuke brought quick response from the War Department. By March 1, 1946, it had admitted in communications to overseas theaters that exchange controls in many instances had not been adequately administered and that some method had to be adopted which would completely block the transfer of local currency arising from sources other than pay and allowances. In these same communications, the War Department outlined the Treasury's proposal, but did not mention joint payment in both scrip and local currencies. Evidently, the War Department thought any break with its practice of paying in indigenous money should be complete. The features of scrip stressed in the communications were (1) the non-acceptance of scrip from unauthorized personnel (scrip finding its way into black markets would be irredeemable by the local population) and (2) the non-reconversion of local currencies into dollar credits. Any amount of scrip could be exchanged for local funds, but once exchanged, it could not be reconverted. By collecting through such official channels as finance offices, Army post offices, and post exchanges *only* what it had disbursed—United States-issued scrip—the Army would have an effective safeguard against any further overdraft. If soldiers acquired scrip from civilians in the black market and converted it into dollar credits, there would be no overdraft since the scrip had been originally issued by the

United States Army and was therefore supported by appropriated funds.[3]

Whereas the American government sought to protect its financial interests through a scrip currency only after it had sustained alarming deficits, the German government had taken a more realistic approach to the problem. From the outbreak of the war, the *Wehrmacht* used a non-convertible currency issued by the government in all occupied territories. This currency, *Reichskreditkassenscheine* (Reich credit treasury notes), was printed in denominations of .5, 1, 2, 5, 20, and 50 marks. When the *Wehrmacht* entered any foreign country, it issued decrees making *Reichskreditkassenscheine* legal tender at a specified exchange rate with the indigenous currency. The ratio was usually the pre-invasion rate between reichsmarks and the local money. German troops received their pay in *Reichskreditkassenscheine,* and since the currency was legal tender only in the occupied areas, the soldiers had to spend their money there or forfeit its value upon returning to Germany.

After January 1, 1945, the *Wehrmacht* adopted another military currency, the *Verrechnungsscheine* (no literal translation is meaningful, but idiomatically, payment orders or credit notes), which was denominated in 1, 5, 10, and 50 marks. It was used when troops were moving from one country to another but not as legal tender in Germany or occupied lands. German soldiers' currency was converted into *Verrechnungsscheine* before they moved into another country. After their arrival it would be converted to the local currency or *Reichskreditkassenscheine.* The *Verrechnungsscheine,* then, were comparable to the American Army's military payment orders. By using these non-convertible occupation currencies, the German government effectively transferred the total cost of the occupation to the defeated country.[4]

Differing from the German practice, the Japanese Army used military scrip backed by the Bank of Japan in the areas it occupied. It was denominated in the units of the conquered countries, such as Netherlands East Indies military guilders, Burmese military rupees, and Philippine military pesos, and circulated along with the indigenous currency. After the Japanese occupation became stable, the Army called in all currency in circulation and issued a new military scrip denominated in yen. Thus, the occupied territories were incorporated in the yen bloc, and all currency clearing was done in Tokyo.[5]

When the War Department seriously contemplated converting to scrip, it requested the reactions of overseas theaters to the feasibility of adopting scrip and to any possible drawbacks connected therewith. These included the disciplinary aspect of soldiers using scrip in the black market (although any involvement could not affect appropriated funds since only Army-issued scrip would be acceptable in official channels) and any possible implications for morale. The latter might arise if soldiers found themselves temporarily without local currency and unable to get to a finance office to make conversions.[6]

The overseas commands with serious currency control problems were unanimously in favor of scrip. Colonel Harold S. Ruth, fiscal director of the Pacific command, thought that scrip would "more effectively accomplish the desires of the Treasury and War Departments, simplify the whole currency control program, and eliminate many onerous aspects of the present system." [7] Colonel Ralph A. Koch, postwar fiscal director for the European theater, advocated scrip since it would give the theater exclusive control of the currency it was using to pay troops. He suggested to the theater G-1 that the scrip could be simply a dollar bill overstamped with "Germany," similar to the Hawaiian overstamp dollars, or a note especially designed for the purpose.[8] The European theater G-1, on the basis of the fiscal director's recommendation and the theater's almost $10,000,000 overdraft in February, 1946, termed scrip "essential" if the theater were ever going to balance its budget.[9]

Those theaters whose currency control problems were slight uniformly opposed the introduction of scrip. The Middle East command contended that the administrative difficulty connected with conversion to scrip would outweigh by far any advantages to be gained in the Middle East. It suggested a worldwide application of currency control books.[10] The Mediterranean theater likewise complained. It said there were insufficient finance department personnel in the theater to make such exchanges. For some indescribable reason, the Mediterranean theater thought scrip would not be as effective as the currency control books! [11] The India-Burma theater opposed scrip because it had only 19,000 men and was phasing out on June 30, 1946.[12]

The civil affairs division of the War Department special staff favored the Treasury's proposal to institute scrip. It reasoned that if soldiers knew they could not convert local currencies into dollar credits, they would have much less desire to accumulate sizeable quantities. Since the demand for local currencies had kept foreign economies constantly inflated, the cessation of this demand would have a stabilizing influence.[13]

Any foreknowledge black-market operators had of a change in methods of currency control would cause them to intensify their efforts in amassing maximum profits before the change occurred. Therefore, the War Department's communiqués to overseas commands, and the commands' replies were classified as SECRET. Yet, in the vigorous tradition of American journalism, an enterprising reporter for the New York *Herald-Tribune* got the news. On March 9, 1946, the paper carried a story announcing that the European theater was considering issuing a scrip currency that would be valid only in official channels.[14]

When the War Department received replies from the large overseas theaters favoring scrip, it called a conference for April. Attending were fiscal and staff representatives from the European theater, the Mediterranean theater, and the Pacific command, as well as War Department representatives from G-1, the operations division, the budget division, and the Office of the Chief of Finance. The consensus of the conference was that scrip should be introduced as quickly as possible. The chairman of the conference, Colonel Pforzheimer, therefore proposed to the budget officer that the War Department adopt a scrip. Pforzheimer felt its greatest advantage was that its circulation within the military enclave would be exclusively controlled by the Army.[15] His thinking about the Army's currency control objectives had matured since August, 1945, when he went on record as being opposed to anything similar to *Reichskreditkassenscheine*.[16]

A month and a half after the budget officer received the conference's recommendation, he proposed to the Secretary of War that the production of a scrip currency called "military payment certificates" begin. He also mentioned that around August 1, 1946, the British Army planned to adopt a similar scrip, termed "canteen money," to regulate excess conversions arising in its zones of occupied Germany and Austria. He further proposed that the Pacific command be allowed to run a trial on scrip with the type A yen. If this experiment proved successful, the War Department would adopt scrip for other overseas commands. Robert P. Patterson, Secretary of War, approved both proposals.[17]

When the occupation of Japan and Korea began, the Pacific command had ample stocks of type B and type A yen available. Type B was designated for use in Japan, and the latter, in Korea. It took the Pacific command only two days to discover that there was no need for type A yen in Korea, since Bank of Chosen notes were plentiful. Therefore, type A yen was completely withdrawn from circulation in the Far East. When the War Department began thinking seriously about introducing scrip, it decided to experiment with this yen, which had characteristics of the proposed scrip. The military yen was distinctively marked, so it could be distinguished easily from indigenous yen, and the American government was the only source of supply. General MacArthur gave his "hearty concurrence" to the experiment, and the War Department and the Pacific command set July 19, 1946, as the date for introduction of type A yen. The budget officer then informed the Secretary of the Treasury of the experiment scheduled for the Far East. If the trial proved a success, the War Department intended to introduce military payment certificates in the European theater and the Mediterranean theater, as well as in the Pacific command.[18]

The details of this proposed experiment, as in the case of the War Department's request in March for the reaction of overseas theaters to scrip, were fully described in the American press. On June 25, 1946, the New York *Times* ran a story about the military currency to be adopted in the Pacific command "soon." The account cited Colonel Harold S. Ruth as the source of its information, all of which was entirely correct. The only omission in the story was the nomenclature of the currency to be used.[19]

The command's experiment with type A yen began on July 19 with the implementation of Circular 52. This directive stipulated that type A yen would be the only currency to circulate within official channels of the Pacific command and would be used exclusively for disbursements and collections. Finance officers could exchange type A yen for Imperial yen, but they would not reconvert indigenous yen back into dollar credits or type A yen.[20]

On the day of the conversion from type B to type A yen, all Army post offices, post exchanges, and quartermaster sales stores were closed to business. Representatives from these agencies took their Imperial and type B yen to finance offices and converted them to type A yen on a one-for-one basis. Enlisted men, along with officers and War Department civilian employees, exchanged their funds through their organization commanders. When presenting these funds for exchange, commanding officers had to execute the following statement: "I certify that I have personally inquired into and examined the source of funds herewith presented for exchange into Type "A" military yen and have determined that these funds were legitimately obtained as payment of pay and allowances from a finance officer of the United States Army or other legitimate sources and were not obtained from sale of property, black market operations, or other illicit sources." [21]

Type A yen was successful immediately; the conversion of black-market profits into dollar credits was brought to an abrupt end. With the Army issuing the only legal tender circulating in official channels and with disbursing officers collecting only what was being issued, the possibility of an overdraft was nil. By August 2, 1946, General Richards was so impressed with the success of the Far Eastern experiment that he recommended the adoption of scrip in all overseas commands to the Secretary of War. He further suggested that a target date for the conversion to scrip in the European and Mediterranean theaters be established between September 10 and 20, and in the Pacific command, between September 20 and 30.[22] On August 7 the Secretary of War approved military payment certificates for these three theaters, and the commanders were requested to designate the earliest date when scrip could be introduced in their theaters.[23]

Soon after the Secretary of War approved the production of the military payment certificates in June, 1946, the Bureau of Engraving and Printing began its task of designing and printing the new currency. Bills were produced in the following denominations: $10.00, $5.00, $1.00, 50¢, 25¢, 10¢, and 5¢. Because the scrip was to have full dollar backing, the bureau was obliged to print notes that would be as difficult to counterfeit as the standard American dollar. Consequently, many features to foil counterfeiters were incorporated in the certificates: colored discs similar to those used in traveler's checks were put in the special paper stock; a formula was devised whereby counterfeit serial numbers could be detected; and special inks were used so that even the most inexperienced handler could detect counterfeits immediately when he put them under a fluorescent light.[24] By working extensive overtime, the bureau had the new military payment certificates ready so that the overseas theaters could meet their deadlines.

"Conversion Day" in Europe was September 16, 1946. Before the actual conversions began, some previous arrangements had been made. At 6:00 P.M. on September 14 the European theater had lifted the TOP SECRET classification from "C Day" and had proclaimed a moratorium for all official agencies for September 15.[25] During this period while all monetary business was suspended, men began turning in their funds to personnel officers; the following day, C Day, they began receiving their military payment certificates, series 461, in exchange.[26] In Germany, Great Britain, Austria, Italy, Belgium, Holland, Denmark, Luxembourg, Trieste, France, Switzerland, and North Africa (the west African district of the European theater), all personnel, soldiers and civilians alike, exchanged their legitimately acquired foreign currencies for scrip. Although these twelve areas were affected by the conversion to scrip, this phase of currency control was aimed primarily at Germany, where the Russian-printed Allied military marks had wreaked havoc with the Army's currency control program. The European theater used scrip in countries other than Germany mainly as a matter of uniformity within the command and not through necessity.[27] Approximately $59,000,000 in francs and marks were converted into scrip in France and Germany on C Day.[28]

Conversion Day in the Pacific command, September 30, 1946, was much more routine than that in Europe, since currency control had already been achieved in the Pacific command with the use of type A yen. The conversion actually was made in a two-week period so that there would be a minimum of interference with normal duties, and it should have rightly been termed "C Fortnight." In Japan, Korea, and the Ryukyus, Army post offices, post exchanges, quartermaster sales stores, and other official agencies remained open during the exchange period. Since this conversion was merely from one form of scrip to another, there was no excitement and little interference with normal administrative routine. Troops received their September pay in the new scrip.[29]

After the Army adopted scrip and brought an end to excess conversions, it was able to determine the exact magnitude of its overdraft. The amount as of December 31, 1946, was staggering—$530,775,440. This figure included overdrafts in all the diverse foreign currencies the Army handled in World War II. The ten largest excesses were as follows: $270,909,788 in German marks; $73,037,246 in Japanese, Korean, and Ryukyus yen; $25,783,329 in Austrian schillings; $23,761,269 in Dutch guilders; $19,793,680 in Indian rupees; $19,339,228 in Belgian francs; $11,344,577 in Philippine pesos; $4,146,237 in pounds from England and North Ireland; $3,176,823 in Iranian rials; and $3,141,603 in Czechoslovakian kroner.[30]

Even as the War Department was compiling these distasteful statistics, the Army was quietly beginning to work off this overdraft. The Pacific command began dissipating its excess as soon as it had brought about currency control by making the occupation forces pay for many of the services they had been receiving free of charge from the Japanese government. For the first time in the occupation, American servicemen paid for personal travel on railroads, lodging at rest hotels, and green fees at golf courses; officers' and enlisted men's clubs paid for Japanese employees; and occupation households paid for domestic help. These payments were made not to the individuals furnishing the services nor to the Japanese government, but to the United States Army. The Army was still receiving these services free under the armistice terms, but it was crediting collections for these services against the overdraft. When scrip was collected, the yen equivalent was withdrawn from the excess account.[31] The Pacific command was able, between August 31, 1946, and February 28, 1947, to reduce its overdraft some $10,000,000.[32]

Early in 1947 the War Department decided to make a systematic effort to dissipate the overdraft in all overseas areas. It patterned its plan after that of the Pacific command. The Secretary of War announced formally on March 15, 1947, that the Army was going to spend its excess currencies before it started using dollars from appropriations. The Treasury and Navy departments had concurred in this policy. Currencies from the overdraft would be used for (1) any expenditure an official government agency normally made from appropriated funds, (2) any expenditure by a quasi-official organization or private enterprise operating within and for the Army, and (3) any expenditure made by individual servicemen or War Department civilians. Despite the fact that using the overdraft to pay for official expenditures was contrary to armistice terms, President Truman approved the Secretary of War's policy on May 15, 1947, which proved the timelessness of the maxim, "To the victor belongs the spoils." [33]

The Army's practical application of this policy took many forms. The greatest single reduction of the overdraft occurred when the Army settled Axis prisoner of war accounts with the excess currencies. According to the Geneva convention of 1929, to which the United States government was a signatory, prisoners of war are entitled to certain payments. German and Japanese prisoners of war had accrued dollar credits during their captivity, but when their accounts were settled, they were paid from the excess funds and their dollar credits, amounting to some $150,000,000 were applied against the overdraft.[34] The Army began crediting the dollars collected as rent from servicemen, civilian employees, and official agencies against the deficit. Rental property was being furnished by the occupied countries; consequently, the Army could apply all its rental collections against the overdraft. The Army also began using the overdraft to pay for local goods procured for sale in post exchanges.[35] By employing these and various other methods, the Army had reduced the overdraft to approximately $380,000,000 in June, 1947. In that month the Senate committees on appropriations, banking and currency, and armed services called hearings on occupation currency transactions. The hearings revealed that the Army expected to have dissipated the overdraft by the end of 1948 and that it did not anticipate calling on Congress for an appropriation to liquidate the deficit.[36]

In February, 1947, the British Army had been in a similar position, having had to explain its overdraft to Parliament. It had acquired excess German and Austrian currencies amounting to £58,-000,000, or $232,000,000, in much the same manner as the American Army. British Tommies had sold their canteen goods at inflated prices to civilians and converted their profits into pound credits.[37] The British War Office was able to write off £38,000,000 by debiting a surplus in its general grant from Parliament. Although the War Office did not try to conceal the total amount of its over-draft, it did not inform Parliament of how it had disposed of the £38,000,000. Parliament thought that the extent of the overdraft was the £20,000,000 supplemental appropriation the War Office requested. Although Parliament granted the appropriation, it ex-pressed great indignation that the British Army had permitted such an outrage.[38]

The American Army escaped severe censure from Congress by not requesting a deficit appropriation. Public opinion in the United States had been aroused by the Army's negligence in the realm of currency control, and the Army was wise, therefore, to avoid calling on the taxpayer directly to solve its problems. Of course, had there been no overdraft, the Army would not have needed the normal appropriations against which expenditures from the overdraft were being charged; it would merely have accepted the services required of the defeated powers by terms of the armistice without having to charge members of the military establishment for them. When these charges were collected in scrip, an equivalent amount of the over-draft was liquidated. Those portions of the normal operations of the Army covered by Congressional appropriations but paid for from the overdraft would not have needed to be included in the appropriations. By virtue of their having been included, the tax-payers' cost for supporting the Army was higher. Moreover, the inflation of occupied economies to which the Army's inept currency control methods had contributed caused the Army to pay higher prices for local expenditures. The Army did not return any unused appropriated funds to the Treasury but retained the full amount of the appropriations so that it would have a way of writing off the overdraft. As currency from the overdraft was spent, debit entries were made against the normal appropriations. Consequently, the taxpayer was indirectly bearing the burden while the Army liqui-dated its deficit. Through persistent efforts, the Army was able to maintain its dissipation schedule. Of the $530,775,440 excess that existed on December 31, 1946, only $10,000,000 remained in disbursing officers' accounts two years later. The War Department considered this amount to be a reasonable working balance.[39]

The most encouraging factor emerging from this experience is that the Army, having found the Treasury's advice sound, used scrip as long as there existed a pressing need for currency control. Scrip was withdrawn in Germany, France, and Italy on May 27, 1958, and troops in those areas began receiving pay in dollars. By 1958 so many American tourists were spending dollars in Europe that there appeared little reason to discriminate against soldiers stationed there, and the respective governments no longer feared the inflationary effects of soldiers' dollars on their economies. The decision to abandon scrip and to institute dollar payments was made with the full approval of the European governments concerned. Indeed, they welcomed the dollar! It is significant that when scrip was abandoned, the Army did not revert to its wartime policy of paying in foreign currencies that could then be converted into dollar credits. It chose, rather, to deal in a currency emanating solely from the United States government. As long as the American government continues to shun dollars as a concession to the wishes of some foreign governments, the Army should unquestionably abide by a dollar-denominated scrip over which it maintains exclusive control. This practice is being followed currently (1964) in Korea, Japan, Libya, and Cyprus.

If one subscribes to the "big bang" philosophy that has haunted American thinking—and that of all civilized men—since Hiroshima, any discussion of currency control in a future war would be purely academic. On the other hand, if the United States should get into another full-scale war fought according to the pre-Hiroshima conventions, the Army would have two main uses for currency in any foreign area—to pay commercial bills and to pay its personnel. For the payment of commercial obligations, the Army could use standard dollars if it wanted to procure goods and services expeditiously and was not concerned with the resulting inflation of the local economy. A *Reichskreditkassenscheine* type of currency could also be used if the Army did not want to use dollars or a discredited local currency. But if locally denominated currencies such as the Allied military mark or the Imperial yen still command the confidence of the people, it would be simpler to maintain them.

For currency control among its personnel, the Army should plan to use a dollar-denominated scrip for pay purposes. The World War II experience has demonstrated that scrip is effective in preventing an overdraft as well as in protecting foreign economies from the inflationary attributes of the standard American dollar. It is the only practical solution to the problem—a solution learned at great cost.

Notes | BLACK-MARKET MONEY

Chapter 1

1 Memo for the President from the Secretaries of State, Treasury, War and Navy (n.d.), World War II Records Division, Office of Military Records, National Archives and Records Service, Alexandria, Virginia; hereinafter cited as World War II Records Division. Minutes of meeting held in [John J.] McCloy's office February 1, 1944, World War II Records Division; Minutes of meeting held in McCloy's office, January 6, 1944, World War II Records Division.

2 Personal transfer accounts were a means of sending money from an overseas theater to the United States at no cost to the soldier. Soldier's deposits were savings accounts for enlisted men which paid 4 per cent annual interest.

3 John D. Millett, *The Organization and Role of the Army Service Forces* (Washington, 1954), 349–50.

4 See Walter Rundell, Jr., "Invasion Currency: A U. S. Army Fiscal Problem in World War II," *The Southwestern Social Science Quarterly*, XLIII (1962), 142–51, for a discussion of the Army's issuance and use of currencies denominated in the monetary units of occupied nations. Of interest also is Walter E. Spahr's *Allied Military Currency* (New York, 1943), which offers a vigorous inquiry into the constitutionality of the Treasury's issuing military currency.

5 Lt. Col. Paul A. Feyereisen, "Foreign Currency Balances of

United States Army After World War II—Their Utilization," Plans and Policy Office, Office of Army Comptroller (September 7, 1949), 3, World War II Records Division.

6   The official rate of exchange was 20-to-1, whereas the free-market rate sometimes went as high as 1700-to-1.

7   Robert P. Patterson for the Secretary of War, August 5, 1942 (Memo), World War II Records Division.

8   Joint Statement of the War and Treasury Departments, January 2, 1945, General Services Administration, Federal Records Center, Kansas City, Missouri; hereinafter cited as Federal Records Center.

9   Maj. Gen. J. A. Ulio to Commanders, Theaters of Operations, *et al.*, July 14, 1944, AG 123 OB-S-E-M, Federal Records Center.

10 A. J. Rehe to Commanding General, European theater, November 4, 1942, AG 242 (10-27-42) OB-S-A, Federal Records Center.

11 Rehe to Commander-in-Chief, southwest Pacific area, November 4, 1942, AG 242 (10-27-42) OB-S-A, Federal Records Center.

12 Rehe to Commanding General, European theater, November 4, 1942, Federal Records Center.

13 Col. B. M. Fitch to the Adjutant General, December 5, 1942, AG 242 (11-4-42) CS, Federal Records Center.

14 Gen. Douglas MacArthur to the Right Honorable John Curtin, July 31, 1944, Federal Records Center; Fitch to the Adjutant General, July 31, 1944, AG 242 (July 14, 1944) DCS, Federal Records Center.

15 Brig. Gen. (Ret.) N. H. Cobbs, "Finance Department, European Theater of Operations," January, 1946 (MS in the Office of the Chief of Finance, Washington, D.C.), p. 15.

16 Total Disbursements and Analysis of Monthly Disposition of Military Pay to Troops, Advance Section, Communications Zone, European Theater, in "The History of the Fiscal Section," Federal Records Center.

17 From charts, "MTOUSA, Disposition of Pay—U. S. Army Personnel, 1944–45," Federal Records Center.

Frank A. Southard, Jr., a financial adviser to the Mediterranean theater and economics professor at Cornell University after the war, contended that compulsory withholding of soldiers' pay could not reduce the amount of pay retained overseas any more effectively than this savings program. Contrary to many observers, he maintained that the inflationary impact of troop spending was "easily exaggerated." Moreover, he declared that "neither the troops themselves nor American public opinion would tolerate a pay-withholding system which limited troop pay-withdrawals for local expenditures to as small a percentage as this [18 per cent]." Quoted in Frank A. Southard, Jr., "Some European Currency and Exchange Experiences: 1943–1946," *Essays in International Finance* (Princeton, 1946), 12.

18 Gen. Douglas MacArthur to the Right Honorable John Curtin, July 31, 1944, Federal Records Center; Fitch to the Adjutant General, July 31, 1944, AG 242 (July 14, 1944) DCS, Federal Records Center.
19 "History of the Services of Supply, China–Burma–India Theater, Appendix 13, Fiscal and Finance Operations, 28 February 1942 to 24 October 1944" (MS in the Office of the Chief of Military History, Washington, D.C.), pp. 11–13.
20 Late in the war the China–Burma–India theater was split into the China theater and India–Burma theater.
21 Lt. Col. A. J. Gricius to All Units Concerned, February 6, 1945, Federal Records Center.

Chapter 2

1 "History of Fiscal and Finance Activities in the Middle Pacific from 7 December 1941 to 2 September 1945" (MS in the Office of the Chief of Military History), 21–22.
2 Brig. Gen. W. E. Farthing to Commanding General, Seventh Air Force, July 19, 1942, Federal Records Center.
3 G-2 Information Bulletin No. 2, Headquarters, United States Army Forces in the South Pacific Area, January 11, 1943, Federal Records Center.
4 Administrative Bulletin 4, South Pacific Base Command, September 17, 1944, World War II Records Division.
5 Interview with Col. B. J. Tullington, Office of the Chief of Finance, August 2, 1955.
6 Maj. Edgar D. Upstill, Report of Reconnaissance, Tongan Islands, July 22, 1942, Federal Records Center.
7 "Tenth Army Action Report, Report of Operations in the Ryukyus Campaign," Federal Records Center.
8 Chang Kai-Ngau, *The Inflationary Spiral, The Experience in China, 1939–1950* (Cambridge, Mass., 1958), 52, 301.
9 "History of Fiscal and Finance Operations, Services of Supply, China–Burma–India Theater, from Activation Through 31 December 1944" (MS in Federal Records Center), January 15, 1945; hereinafter cited as "History of Fiscal and Finance Operations." Col. E. J. Bean to Miss Margaree Lott, March 22, 1945, World War II Records Division.
10 "History of Fiscal and Finance Operations."
11 Chang, *The Inflationary Spiral,* 302.
12 *Ibid.,* 52.
13 Robert P. Patterson, and H. H. Kung, November 25, 1944 (Memorandum of Agreement), Federal Records Center.
14 Lt. Gen. Brehon Somervell to the Secretary of the Treasury, January 3, 1944, World War II Records Division; Memorandum

on Chinese Exchange Situation, May 19, 1944, World War II Records Division.

15 Capt. Robert A. Waidner to Commanding General, Forward Echelon, China–Burma–India theater, February 2, 1943, Federal Records Center.

16 Maj. Gen. A. H. Carter to Assistant Chief of Staff, Operations Division, August 10, 1944, World War II Records Division; M. R. Rutherford, "Commercial and Financial Developments, July 1944," American Consulate General, Kunming, Yunnan, China, August 19, 1944, World War II Records Division; Memo 16, China–Burma–India theater, September 21, 1944, World War II Records Division.

17 Winston S. Churchill, Speech on Dunkirk, House of Commons, June 4, 1940.

18 Col. Ralph Pulsifier to Commanding General, Services of Supply, European theater, *et al.*, April 29, 1943, AG 121.2–0, Federal Records Center.

19 Headquarters, United States Army Forces in the Middle East (USAFIME), Office of the Fiscal Director, Cairo, Egypt, for Commanding General, USAFIME, August 15, 1944 (Memo), F.D. 301, Federal Records Center.

20 Col. R. E. Odell for Commanding General, USAFIME, December 22, 1944 (Memo), F.D. 319.1 (C.F.O.), Federal Records Center.

21 *Ibid.*

22 *Ibid.*

23 Col. Francis H. Oxx to Commanding General, Services of Supply, North African theater of Operations, United States Army (hereinafter cited as North African theater), August 28, 1944, AG 123.7 BPFINS, Federal Records Center.

24 Brig. Gen. Arthur R. Wilson to Commanding General, North African theater, December 3, 1944, AGD 333.1 BMCOS–M, Federal Records Center.

25 Military Attaché Report, May 30, 1944, Report No. 13555, Sub. 6, Sec. 5, United States Currency, World War II Records Division.

26 Maj. Gerald J. Linares to Commanding General, Africa–Middle East theater, April 7, 1945, 123.7, Federal Records Center.

27 Circular 47, North African theater, April 5, 1944, Federal Records Center; Circular No. 16, Persian Gulf command, February 19, 1945, Federal Records Center.

28 Capt. George W. Sparks to Commanding General, Africa–Middle East theater, April 21, 1945, AG 123 BMFIN, Federal Records Center.

29 Technical Intelligence Report No. 671, April 28, 1945, Sub. 29, Troop Pay, World War II Records Division.

30 Division of Monetary Research, U.S. Treasury Department, September 23, 1943 (Memo), World War II Records Division.

31 Gen. Eisenhower to Adjutant General, War Department, Washington, February 1, 1943 (Radio Message), FHAEF 8430, Federal Records Center; Maj. Gen. A. H. Carter for Director, Budget Division, War Department General Staff, thru Chief of Staff, Army Service Forces, February 3, 1945 (Memo), SPFDF, World War II Records Division.

32 Commander-in-Chief to Commanding Generals, Fifth Army, *et al.*, February 1, 1943 (Radio Message), 8428, Federal Records Center.

33 Interview with Lt. Col. T. W. Archer, Office of the Comptroller of the Army, March 3, 1954.

34 Report on White House Conference, from Press Branch, Bureau of Public Relations, War Department, June 13, 1944, World War II Records Division.

35 Minutes of meeting held in McCloy's office February 1, 1944, World War II Records Division; Minutes of meeting held in McCloy's office, January 6, 1944, World War II Records Division.

36 Brig. Gen. R. B. Lovett to Commanding Generals, United Kingdom Base, Communications Zone, March 15, 1945, 123.250.1 OpGa, Federal Records Center.

37 Lt. Col. Richard P. Fisk to Commanding General, U.S. Strategic Air Forces in Europe, *et al.*, February 29, 1944, AG 123.7, OpFD, Federal Records Center.

38 Col. M. F. Moriarty to All Fiscal and Finance Officers, Europe, December 4, 1944, Federal Records Center; Frank J. Wilson to Chief of Finance, March 23, 1943, 000.5 General, World War II Records Division.

39 "History of the Fiscal Section." The communications zone was a rear area where support activities transpired.

40 Gen. Eisenhower to Commanding General, Mediterranean theater, December 31, 1944 (Radio Message), E-81041, Federal Records Center.

41 Brig. Gen. R. B. Lovett to Commanding General, U.S. Strategic Air Forces in Europe, *et al.*, April 19, 1945, AG 123 OpGa, Federal Records Center. See the discussion of the April prohibition against Reichsmarks in Chapter III.

42 Cobbs, "Finance Department, European Theater," 20–23; Col. Ralph A. Koch, Lt. Col. Harold W. Uhrbrock, and Lt. Col. Maynard N. Levenick, "The Activities of the Finance Department in the European Theater of Operations," Study 75, The General Board, United States Forces, European theater, 12, 53–54.

43 Col. R. B. Conner, "Currency Control, European Theater" (MS in the Office of the Chief of Finance), June 19, 1947, FIND 123 (Europe), 7–10. See the discussion in Chapter III of the decline of the fiscal director's influence, pp. 38–39.

Chapter 3

1 Minutes of meeting in McCloy's office April 8, 1944, World War II Records Division.

2 Adjutant General, War Department from Army Service Forces cite SPFDF, to European theater, June 21, 1945 (Radio Message), WAR-20480, World War II Records Division.

3 Col. John J. Dubbelde, Jr. to Civil Affairs Division, War Department General Staff, December 27, 1944, WDSBU 123 (12–18–44), World War II Records Division.

4 Brig. Gen. N. H. Cobbs to Finance Office, XII Corps, September 7, 1944 (Memo), World War II Records Division.

5 Circular 111, Headquarters, North African theater, September 7, 1944, World War II Records Division.

6 Advance Section, Communications Zone to European theater, March 13, 1945 (Radio Message), R-59066, World War II Records Division.

7 Col. R. E. Cummings to Commanding General, European theater, March 21, 1945, AG 121-GNMCK, World War II Records Division; Lt. Col. Walter Sczudlo to Commanding General, European theater, April 13, 1945, 123 (G-1), World War II Records Division; Col. W. G. Caldwell to All Units, Seventh Army, March 21, 1945, AG 123.7, World War II Records Division.

8 Carrier Sheet, Headquarters, European theater, March 18, 1945, World War II Records Division.

9 Carrier Sheet, Headquarters, European theater, April 14, 1945, World War II Records Division.

10 Carrier Sheet, Headquarters, European theater, May 22, 1945, AG 123 OpGa, World War II Records Division.

11 Finance Circular Letter 80, Change No. 3, Headquarters, European theater, Office of the Fiscal Director, April 19, 1945, World War II Records Division; Brig. Gen. R. B. Lovett to Commanding General, U.S. Strategic Air Forces in Europe, *et al.,* April 19, 1945, AG 123 OpGa, World War II Records Division.

12 Lt. Gen. W. B. Smith to Lt. Gen. John C. H. Lee, May 16, 1945, AG 123 OpGa, World War II Records Division.

13 Carrier Sheet, Headquarters, European theater, May 22, 1945, AG 123 OpGa, World War II Records Division.

14 Maj. Gen. George J. Richards, to Headquarters, Communications Zone, European theater, June 7, 1945 (Radio Message), WDSBU 123 Currency (May 25, 1945) 474, World War II Records Division.

15 Office of the Fiscal Director, to Supreme Headquarters, Main Echelon, Versailles, France, June 22, 1945 (Radio Message), World War II Records Division.

16 Office of Military Government, United States, to War Department, January 13, 1947 (Radio Message), CC 7647, in *Occupation Currency Transactions,* Hearings before the Committees on Appropriations, Armed Services, and Banking and Currency, United States Senate (Washington, 1947), 667.

17 Minutes of meeting held in office of the Assistant Secretary of War, May 30, 1945, World War II Records Division.

18 Memo for Record, Maj. T. G. Upton, June 7, 1945, World War II Records Division.

19 Maj. Gen. W. H. Kasten to Finance Office, U.S. Army, New York, N.Y., December 18, 1945, SPFBC 123.7 EC, World War II Records Division; Col. C. K. McAlister to the Fiscal Director, December 26, 1945, World War II Records Division.

20 Koch, Uhrbrock, and Levenick, "The Activities of the Finance Department . . . ," 8.

21 Conner, "Currency Control, European Theater," 7–10. See the discussion of this point on p. 30.

Chapter 4

1 Minutes of meeting held in McCloy's office, January 6, 1944, World War II Records Division.

2 D. W. Bell to A. W. Hall, April 27, 1944 (Treasury Department Inter-Office Communication), World War II Records Division.

3 Whittaker Chambers, *Witness* (New York, 1952), 429.

4 "One Man's Greed," *Time,* LXII (November 23, 1953), 22–24.

5 From Secretary Morgenthau to the Ambassador of the U.S.S.R., August 14, 1944 (Memo), World War II Records Division.

6 Supreme Headquarters, Forward, to War Department, May 24, 1945 (Radio Message), FWD 22319, World War II Records Division; Col. Carl H. Pforzheimer, Jr. to Gen. Richards, May 26, 1945 (Memo), World War II Records Division.

7 Gen. Eisenhower, Supreme Headquarters, Forward, Rheims, France, to War Department, May 24, 1945 (Cable), FWD 22319 VOG 457, World War II Records Division.

8 Army Service Forces, Office of the Fiscal Director, to Headquarters, Communications Zone, European theater, May 28, 1945 (Radio Message), WAR 89396, World War II Records Division.

9 Feyereisen, "Foreign Currency Balances," 3.

10 Lt. Col. Morton P. Fisher to Lt. Gen. Lucius D. Clay, May 30, 1945, Federal Records Center.

11 Maj. E. M. Buckingham, "Report of Operations," Office of the Finance Officer, U.S. Headquarters, Berlin district, May 8, 1945 to September 30, 1945, p. 2, Federal Records Center.

12 Interview with Col. George R. Gretser, Budget and Fiscal Branch, G-2, Department of the Army, March 30, 1954.

13 A. M. Kamarch to Col. Bernstein, August 1, 1945, World War II Records Division.
14 "The First Year of the Occupation," in Occupation Forces in Europe Series, 1945–1946 (MS in the Office of the Chief of Military History), p. 117.
15 Col. Pforzheimer, for the Budget Officer of the War Department, July 29, 1945 (Memo), World War II Records Division.
16 Memo for Record, Col. Pforzheimer, August 3, 1945, World War II Records Division.
17 Circular 45, U.S. Headquarters, Berlin district and headquarters, First Airborne Army, Berlin, August 9, 1945, World War II Records Division.
18 Buckingham, "Report of Operations," 2.
19 "Report of Operations," Berlin District, January–March, 1946, p. 7, Federal Records Center.
20 Stephen F. Sherwin, *Monetary Policy in Continental Western Europe, 1944–1952* ("Wisconsin Commerce Studies," Vol. II, No. 2 [Madison, 1956]), 8, 49.
21 Fred H. Klopstock, "Monetary Reform in Western Germany," *Journal of Political Economy*, LVII (1949), 280.
22 Horst Mendershausen, "Prices, Money and the Distribution of Goods in Postwar Germany," *American Economic Review*, XXXIX (1949), 651.
23 *Ibid.*, 652.
24 *Ibid.*, 653–54.
25 Col. Pforzheimer to Budget Officer of the War Department, August 12, 1945 (Memo), World War II Records Division.
26 Commanding General, European theater, Main, to War Department, September 10, 1945 (Radio Message), S 22572, World War II Records Division.
27 Memo for Record, Col. Pforzheimer, September 27, 1945, World War II Records Division.
    "Net troop pay" represented that portion of American soldiers' pay disbursed in local currencies. The Army requisitioned foreign currency from restored governments to finance its local operations —paying military personnel and purchasing goods and services. It would carefully account for that portion of the requisition used for troop pay and would then reimburse the restored government in this amount, termed net troop pay. Hence, a restored government was not called upon to bear the ultimate burden of meeting the Army's monthly pay rolls. This usage of the American government was far different from the practices of the Third Reich and the Union of Soviet Socialist Republics, both of which transferred the entire cost of occupation onto the occupied economies.
28 Commanding General, European theater, Main, to War Department, September 10, 1945 (Radio Message), S 22572, World War II Records Division.

29 Col. Thomas H. Young to All Major Commands, September 28, 1945, Federal Records Center.
30 Memo for Record, Maj. T. G. Upton, June 7, 1945, World War II Records Division.
31 Brig. Gen. R. B. Lovett to Commanding General, United States Forces in Austria, *et al.*, September 29, 1945, AG 121 GAP-AGO, World War II Records Division; Conner, "Currency Control, European Theater," 13–14.
32 See the discussion of this point on pp. 70–72.
33 Gen. Eisenhower to Adjutant General, War Department Personal for Handy, October 2, 1945 (Radio Message), S 22572, Federal Records Center.
34 War Department to China theater, *et al.*, October 4, 1945 (Radio Message), W 71871, Federal Records Center.
35 Washington (WDCMC SVC 16199) to China theater headquarters, New Delhi, Commander-in-Chief, Army Forces in the Pacific, U.S. Army Forces in the Middle East, Mediterranean theater headquarters, Teheran, October 2, 1945 (Radio Message), W 71871, Federal Records Center.
36 Memo for Record, Col. Pforzheimer, September 27, 1945, World War II Records Division.
37 Twelfth Army Group to European theater, May 5, 1945, Federal Records Center.
38 Conner, "Currency Control, European Theater," 15.
39 Bank for International Settlements, *Italy's Economic and Financial Position in the Summer of 1947* (Basle, 1947), 12, 28, 38, 69.
40 McNarney to Adjutant General, War Department, Washington, May 17, 1945 (Radio Message), F 76997, Federal Records Center.
41 S. J. Keating, Post Office Inspector, to Chief Inspector, Washington, D.C., June 13, 1945, Case No. 28295–8 No. 60, World War II Records Division.
42 "Fixing the Lira Rate," *The Economist* (London), CXLV (July 10, 1943), 54.
43 Frank A. Southard, Jr., *The Finances of European Liberation* (New York, 1946), 40–41.
44 Commanding General, Mediterranean theater, to Commanding Officer, 1419–4Y Operating Location, Athens, Greece, December 20, 1945 (Radio Message), FX 56817, Federal Records Center.
45 Banque de France, *Compte Rendu des Opérations* (Paris, 1947), 6–7.
46 Richard A. Lester spoke emphatically to this point in "International Aspects of Wartime Monetary Experience," in *Essays in International Finance* (Princeton, 1944), 16. He decried the way fixed exchange rates, which inevitably either over- or undervalued currencies, provided incentive for servicemen to engage in the black market. "It seems undesirable for our servicemen and sea-

men to be devoting their attention and energies to such speculative operations, to be making thousands of dollars of undeserved profits from them, and there is little to be said for the speculation in general." To remedy such a situation, Lester advocated a variable exchange rate that would enable the ratio between currencies to keep pace with the general price structure. On the other hand, Frank M. Tamagna in "The Fixing of Foreign Exchange Rates," *Journal of Political Economy,* LII (1945), 62–63, has stated that if any doubt exists about an exchange rate, "it is better to err on the side of a rate which may involve an overvaluation of the local currency." He explains this theory by saying that such a rate would prevent inflation by limiting the amount of cash in soldiers' hands and by keeping down local prices. In addition, it would have a salutary psychological effect on the natives by bolstering confidence in their currency.

47   Col. Pforzheimer for Gen. Richards, December 26, 1944 (Memo), World War II Records Division.

48   Robert P. Patterson for McCloy, March 23, 1945 (Memo), World War II Records Division.

49   See the discussion of this point on p. 25.

50   Memo, Col. E. C. Bomar, August 22, 1945, WDSBU 123.7, World War II Records Division; Adjutant General, War Department to European theater REAR, August 28, 1945 (Radio Message), WX-55880, World War II Records Division.

51   Gen. Eisenhower to Commanding Generals, United States Forces in Austria, Theater Service Forces, European theater, *et al.,* August 20, 1945, Federal Records Center.

52   War Department Budget Division to Headquarters, India–Burma theater, December 24, 1945 (Radio Message), WARX 87856, WARX 87857, Federal Records Center.

53   Col. H. L. Leighton, "VI Corps History," Headquarters VI Corps, Office of the Finance Officer, May 11–31, 1945, Federal Records Center. This document has obviously been dated incorrectly, for it describes events happening seven months after its date.

54   Interview with Dr. Robert W. Coakley, Office of the Chief of Military History, March 31, 1954.

55   *Report on House Resolution 150, Appendix A,* signed Henry L. Stimson, Scretary of War, April 28, 1945 (Washington, 1945), 1.

56   In World War I the quartermaster corps handled the Army's fiscal affairs.

57   Col. I. L. Hunt, *American Military Government of Occupied Germany, 1919–1920, Report of the Officer in Charge of Civil Affairs, Third Army and American Forces in Germany,* March 4, 1920 (n.p., 1920), 203–204.

Chapter 5

1 Circular 67, General Headquarters, U.S. Army Forces in the Pacific, September 10, 1945, World War II Records Division.

2 Commander-in-Chief, Army Forces in the Pacific to Commander-in-Chief, Army Forces in the Pacific ADVANCE, Commanding General, Sixth Army, *et al.,* October 27, 1945 (Radio Message), Federal Records Center.

3 Commander-in-Chief, Army Forces in the Pacific ADVANCE, to Commanding General, Sixth Army pass to Finance Officer, *et al.,* November 6, 1945 (Radio Message), CAS-54304, Federal Records Center.

4 Circular 127, General Headquarters, U.S. Army Forces in the Pacific, December 12, 1945, Federal Records Center.

5 Hyoye Ouchi, *Financial and Monetary Situation in Post-War Japan* (New York, 1947), 3.

6 Mendershausen, "Prices, Money and the Distribution of Goods in Postwar Germany," 652.

7 Ouchi, *Financial and Monetary Situation in Post-War Japan,* 7, 17.

8 Commander-in-Chief, Army Forces in the Pacific to Commanding General, Sixth Army, *et al.,* October 18, 1945 (Radio Message), 180153 Z, Federal Records Center; Styler to Commanding General, Okinawa Base Command, October 30, 1945 (TWX), 311.23, Federal Records Center.

9 Col. J. B. Rothnie to Fiscal Director, Army Service Forces, October 30, 1945, FL 123, World War II Records Division.

10 "GI Riches in Japan May Not Get Home," New York *Times,* October 21, 1945, p. 28.

11 Fiscal Director, Army Forces in the Pacific, to G-4, Army Forces in the Pacific, May 14, 1946 (Memo), World War II Records Division.

12 Maj. Gen. Richards to the Secretary of War, April 22, 1947, World War II Records Division; Interview with Col. Paul A. Feyereisen, Office of the Comptroller of the Army, August 24, 1955.

13 Fiscal Director, Army Forces in the Pacific, to G-4, Army Forces in the Pacific, May 14, 1946 (Memo), World War II Records Division.

14 Col. Harold S. Ruth to the author, August 15, 1955; Interview with Gordon D. Osborn, Bureau of the Budget, August 24, 1955.

15 Col. Harold S. Ruth, "Currency Control, United States Army Forces, Pacific, 1945–1946," October 2, 1951 (MS in the Office of the Chief of Finance).

16　See pp. 36–38, for a discussion of the War Department's attitude toward currency control.

17　Chang, *The Inflationary Spiral,* 69–70.

18　*Ibid.,* 132, 151–52.

19　Disbursing Information No. 27, China theater, September 19, 1945, Federal Records Center.

20　Lt. Col. Sylvio L. Bousquin to Commanding General, Army Air Force, China theater, *et al.,* September 10, 1945, AG 123, Federal Records Center.

21　War Department Chief of Staff to Manila, Commander-in-Chief, Pacific Ocean area, *et al.,* September, 1945 (Radio Message), WARX 60466, Federal Records Center.

Chapter 6

1　See the discussion of the introduction of type A yen on pp. 85–86.

2　See p. 87, for the account of the European theater's adoption of scrip currency.

3　Maj. Gen. Richards for Col. Pforzheimer, July 20, 1945 (Memo), World War II Records Division.

4　Memo for Record, Col. Pforzheimer, August 3, 1945, World War II Records Division.

5　Col. Pforzheimer to Budget Office, War Department, August 12, 1945 (Memo), World War II Records Division.

6　Maj. Gen. J. M. Bevans to the Chief of Staff, August 29, 1945 (Memo), World War II Records Division.

7　Brig. Gen. R. B. Lovett to Commanding Generals, United States Forces in Austria, *et al.,* September 29, 1945, Ag 121 GAP-AGO, World War II Records Division.

8　Col. Pforzheimer for Budget Division, War Department, December 5, 1945 (Memo), World War II Records Division.

9　"Army Accused of Subterfuge on Censorship," New York *Herald-Tribune,* November 5, 1945.

10　"Army Will Not Tell Disbursals in Europe," New York *Times,* November 1, 1945.

11　" 'Safe' Money Pours in at Berlin APO," *Stars and Stripes* (London) November 1, 1945.

12　War Department Budget Division for Commanding General, European Theater, Main, October 23, 1945 (Radio Message), War 78098, World War II Records Division.

13　Commanding General, European theater, to War Department, October 27, 1945 (Radio Message), S 29485, World War II Records Division.

14　*Ibid.*

15 Circular 139, Headquarters, European theater, October 10, 1945, Federal Records Center.
16 Fiscal Director, Army Forces in the Pacific, to G-4, Army Forces in the Pacific, May 14, 1946 (Memo), World War II Records Division.
17 "Currency Control," in Occupation Forces in Europe Series, 1945–1946 (MS in the Office of the Chief of Military History) pp. 26–27; Conner, "Currency Control, European Theater," 16–18; Interview with Dr. Robert W. Coakley, March 31, 1954; Col. P. W. Brown to Col. Barnes, February 13, 1946 (Memo), World War II Records Division.
18 "Historical Report of Operations," Chanor Base Section, 1946, pp. 18–19, Federal Records Center.
19 Internal Route Slip, Headquarters European theater, signed Maj. Gen. Carter B. Magruder, Chief of Staff, December 27, 1945, World War II Records Division.
20 Interview with Lt. Col. Delavan C. Clos, February 15, 1954.
21 Interview with Col. George R. Gretser, March 30, 1954.
22 War Department to Commander-in-Chief, Army Forces in the Pacific, December 19, 1945 (Radio Message) WCL 29791, Federal Records Center.
23 Circular 10, Headquarters, Mediterranean theater, January 17, 1946, World War II Records Division; Brig. Gen. L. S. Ostrander to the Adjutant General, January 11, 1946, AG 121 GAP-AGO, World War II Records Division.
24 Analysis and Disposition of Military Pay in Foreign Theaters of Operations, European Theater, Period from February 1, 1946 to February 28, 1946, World War II Records Division.
25 Harriman to Secretary of State, May 16, 1946 (Radio Message), 5204, World War II Records Division.
26 "Report of Operations," Berlin District, January–March, 1946, p. 7, Federal Records Center.
27 G-1 Morale Branch, European theater, to G-1 Special Activities, March 4, 1946 (Memo), World War II Records Division.
28 "Reveille Ordered for Troops," New York *Times,* April 28, 1946, p. 18 L.
29 Raymond Daniell, "Easy Profits Play Role in GI Laxity," New York *Times,* April 28, 1946, p. 18 L.
30 Memo, Col. P. W. Brown, February 13, 1946, World War II Records Division.
31 Circular 50, Headquarters, European theater, April 15, 1946, Federal Records Center.
32 Circular 142, Berlin district, July 3, 1946, Federal Records Center.
33 "The First Year of the Occupation," 124.
34 Conner, "Currency Control, European Theater," 19.
35 Analysis and Disposition of Military Pay in Foreign Theaters of

Operations, European Theater, Period from February 1, 1946 to February 28, 1946, World War II Records Division.

36 Maj. Gen. J. M. Bevans to the Chief of Staff, April 4, 1946. World War II Records Division.

37 Circular 82, Headquarters, European theater, June 3, 1946, Federal Records Center; McNarney, to Office of Military Government, United States, July 11, 1946 (Radio Message), S-6944, Federal Records Center.

38 McNarney to Adjutant General, War Department, July 11, 1946 (Radio Message), S-6944, Federal Records Center.

39 Commanding General, European theater to United States Forces in Austria, United States Army in the Far East, Office of Military Government, United States, *et al.,* August 5, 1946 (Radio Message), S 1173, World War II Records Division; War Department Chief of Staff to Commanding General, European theater, July 24, 1946 (Radio Message), WARX 95562, World War II Records Division.

Chapter 7

1 The military payment order was somewhat analogous to a cashier's check, although it was devised specifically to obviate the need for a Treasury check as a means of transferring funds. A soldier overseas or en route to a foreign station could turn in excess cash at an Army finance office and receive a military payment order for the surrendered funds. At any later time he could go to a finance office and redeem it for currency. This was a great convenience to troops moving through occupied territories.

2 Fred M. Vinson to the Secretary of War, February 18, 1946, World War II Records Division.

3 War Department Budget Division to Commanding Generals, European theater, Mediterranean theater, Army Forces in the Pacific, *et al.,* March 1, 1946 (Radio Message), WARX 99066, World War II Records Division; War Department Budget Division to Commanding General, Africa-Middle East theater, *et al.,* March 4, 1946 (Radio Message), WARS 99066, World War II Records Division; War Department Budget Division to Commanding General, China theater, March 6, 1946 (Radio Message), WAR 99651, World War II Records Division.

4 Hans J. Dernburg, "Currency Techniques in Military Operations," April 11, 1945, Federal Records Center; Cmdr. Frank A. Southard, Jr. to Fiscal Director, May 31, 1945 (Memo), G-5/123.9, Federal Records Center.

5 Henry Simon Bloch and Bert F. Hoselitz, *Economics of Military Occupation* (Chicago, 1944), 138.

6   War Department Budget Division to Commanding Generals, European theater, Mediterranean theater, Army Forces in the Pacific, *et al.*, March 1, 1946 (Radio Message), WARX 99066, World War II Records Division; War Department Budget Division to Commanding General, Africa-Middle East theater, *et al.*, March 4, 1946 (Radio Message), WARS 99066, World War II Records Division; War Department Budget Division to Commanding General, China theater, March 6, 1946 (Radio Message), WAR 99651, World War II Records Division.

7   Col. Harold S. Ruth to Chief of Staff, Army Forces in the Pacific, March 6, 1946, World War II Records Division.

8   Col. R. A. Koch to G-1, European theater, March 6, 1946 (Memo), World War II Records Division.

9   Maj. Gen. J. M. Bevans to the Chief of Staff, April 4, 1946, World War II Records Division.

10   U.S. Army Forces in the Middle East, to War Department, March 6, 1946 (Radio Message), N2022, World War II Records Division.

11   Commanding General, Mediterranean theater to War Department, March 15, 1946 (Radio Message), F 62835, World War II Records Division.

12   Commanding General, India-Burma Theater to War Department Budget Division, March 8, 1946 (Radio Message), CRA 5242, World War II Records Division.

13   Brig. Gen. George F. Schulgen to Budget Division, War Department General Staff, March 11, 1946, World War II Records Division.

14   Edwin Hartrich, "Army in Germany Seeks to Cut Loss from Soviet-Printed Scrip, May Issue Currency Valid Only for Authorized Personnel in U.S. Zone," New York *Herald-Tribune,* March 9, 1946.

15   Col. Pforzheimer for the Budget Officer of the War Department, April 27, 1946 (Memo), World War II Records Division; Staff Study on the Major Considerations Affecting the Legality of the Use of a Single Special Medium of Exchange Within the Military Enclave, Prepared by: Chief, Foreign Financial Branch, Budget Division, War Department Special Staff, April 27, 1946, World War II Records Division.

16   Memo for Record, Col. Pforzheimer, August 3, 1945, World War II Records Division; see p. 48, for further information on Colonel Pforzheimer's philosophy of currency control.

17   Maj. Gen. Richards for the Secretary of War, June 14, 1946 (Memo), WDSBU 123.7 (April 10, 1945) 533, World War II Records Division; Maj. Gen. Richards to the Secretary of the Treasury, July 3, 1946, WDSBU 123 Currency (September 7, 1945) 2250, World War II Records Division.

18   Col. Ruth to Col. Pforzheimer, June 16, 1946, World War II

Records Division; Maj. Gen. Richards to the Secretary of the Treasury, July 3, 1946, World War II Records Division.

19 Lindesay Parrott, "Occupation Money Ordered in Japan," New York *Times,* June 25, 1946.

20 Circular 52, General Headquarters, U.S. Army Forces in the Pacific, June 18, 1946, Federal Records Center; Commander-in-Chief, Army Forces in the Pacific to Commanding General, Eighth Army, *et al.,* July 3, 1946 (Radio Message), 2XO6566, Federal Records Center.

21 Commander-in-Chief, Army Forces in the Pacific to Commanding General, Eighth Army, *et al.,* July 3, 1946 (Radio Message), 2XO6566, Federal Records Center; "Administrative History, Office of the Fiscal Director," General Headquarters, U.S. Army Forces in the Pacific, April 6, 1945 to December 31, 1946 (MS in the Office of the Chief of Military History).

22 Maj. Gen. Richards for the Secretary of War, August 2, 1946 (Memo), WDSBU 125 (April 10, 1946), World War II Records Division.

23 War Department Budget Division to Commander-in-Chief, Army Forces in the Pacific, Commanding General, European theater, Commanding General, Mediterranean theater, August 7, 1946 (Cable) WARX 96748, World War II Records Division.

24 War Department Chief of Staff to Commanding General, European theater, July 24, 1946 (Radio Message), WARX 95562, World War II Records Division; Commander-in-Chief, Army Forces in the Pacific to Commanding Generals, Eighth Army, XXIV Corps, Army Forces in the western Pacific, *et al.,* August 20, 1946 (Radio Message), World War II Records Division.

25 Col. George F. Herbert to Commanding Generals, United States Forces in Austria, Western Base Section, *et al.,* September 7, 1946, Ag 123.7 GAP-AGA, World War II Records Division.

26 "Currency Control," in Occupation Forces in Europe Series, 1945–46, 55.

27 FINEF for Fiscal Director, DUSAME, *et al.,* n.d. (Radio Message), AMSME No. WCL 44099, Federal Records Center.

28 "The First Year of Occupation," in Occupation in Europe Series, 1945–46, 123.

29 Commanding General, XXIV Corps to Commanding Generals, 6th Division, 7th Division, U.S. Army Military Government in Korea, Korean Base Command, August 28, 1946 (Radio Message), TFFIS 260, World War II Records Division; Washington (WDSBU) to Commanding General, Eighth Army, *et al.,* September 27, 1946 (Radio Message), WCL 46998, Federal Records Center; Circular 90, General Headquarters, U.S. Army Forces in the Pacific, September 30, 1946, Federal Records Center.

30 Feyereisen, "Foreign Currency Balances," 3.

31 Col. Ruth to the author, August 15, 1955; Commander-in-Chief,

Army Forces in the Pacific, to War Department for War Department Budget Division, July 24, 1946 (Radio Message), C63402, World War II Records Division.

32 Maj. Gen. Richards to the Secretary of War, April 22, 1947, World War II Records Division.

33 Feyereisen, "Foreign Currency Balances," 7, 22; Memo of Understanding for the President, signed John W. Snyder, Robert P. Patterson, and Dean Acheson, approved Harry S. Truman, May 15, 1947, World War II Records Division.

34 For a fuller discussion of the monetary settlement made for repatriated prisoners of war, see Walter Rundell, Jr., "Paying the POW in World War II," *Military Affairs,* XXII (1958) 127–28.

35 Maj. Gen. M. G. White to Maj. Gen. Richards, April 25, 1947, Inclosure No. 1, WDSBU 125 (March 15, 1947) 9294, World War II Records Division.

36 *Occupation Currency Transactions,* 3; Feyereisen, "Foreign Currency Balances," 4.

37 *The Parliamentary Debates* (London, Her Majesty's Stationery Office), February 18, 1947, p. 11 F14.

38 Report, Lt. Col. Feyereisen and James R. Brooks, April 8, 1947, World War II Records Division; Memo for the Files, April 3, 1947, World War II Records Division.

39 Feyereisen, "Foreign Currency Balances," 38.

Bibliography | BLACK-MARKET MONEY

ARCHIVAL MATERIAL

World War II Records Division, Office of Military Records, National Archives and Records Service, Alexandria, Virginia.

General Services Administration, Federal Records Center, Kansas City, Missouri.

Bulletins—War Department, Finance Department, Theaters, Base Sections

Cables—War Departments, Theaters

Carrier Sheets—Theater Headquarters

Charts—Analysis and Disposition of Pay in Foreign Theaters

Circulars—War Department, Finance Department, Theaters, Base Sections

Circular Letters—Finance Department, Theaters, Base Sections

Intelligence Reports—Counterintelligence Corps, Attaché

Inter-Office Communications—Treasury Department

Inter-Staff Routing Slips—Theater Headquarters

Letters (Correspondence Files)—War Department, Treasury Department, Theaters, Base Sections, Armies, Corps, Divisions, Air Forces, Finance Disbursing Sections

Memoranda—War Department, Treasury Department, Finance Department, Theaters

Minutes of Meetings—War Department and Treasury Department Committees

Radio Messages—War Department, Theaters

Reconnaissance Reports

Special Orders—Theaters
Staff Studies—War Department
TWX (Military Telegrams)—Theaters

REPORTS OF OPERATION, FEDERAL RECORDS CENTER

"After Action Report, Annex No. 217, Finance, U.S. Seventh Army, June 1944 to May 1945."

Annual Reports, War Department, Fiscal Year Ended June 30, 1941, Report of the Secretary of War to the President.

Buckingham, E. M., Maj. "Report of Operation." Office of the Finance Officer, U.S. Headquarters, Berlin District, May 8, 1945 to September 30, 1945.

"Historical Report of Operations." Chanor Base Section, Fiscal Station, APO 562, V-E Day to February 20, 1946.

Leighton, H. L., Col. "VI Corps History." Headquarters, VI Corps, Office of Finance Officer, May 11–31, 1945.

"Operational Report." Finance Section, Headquarters, Sixth Army, January 25, 1943 to January 24, 1946.

"Report of Operations." Berlin District, January to March, 1946.

"Report of the Leyte Operation." Sixth Army, October 20, 1944 to December 25, 1944.

"Semi-Annual Report, June 1 to December 31, 1945." Army Forces in the Western Pacific.

Taylor, J. M., 2nd Lt. "Monthly Historical Report." Office of the Finance Officer, Headquarters, Base Three, U.S. Army Services of Supply, APO 923, July, 1944.

"Tenth Army Action Report, Report of Operations in the Ryukyus Campaign, Chapter 11, Staff Section Reports, Section XIX—Finance."

Vance, John R., Col. "Report of Operations, Finance Officer, U.S. Forces in the Philippines, December 8, 1941 to May 6, 1942." September 30, 1944.

MILITARY AND FINANCIAL HISTORIES

"Administrative History, Office of the Fiscal Director," General Headquarters, U.S. Army Forces in the Pacific, April 6, 1945 to December 31, 1946, Office Chief of Military History.

Cobbs, N. H., Brig. Gen. (Ret.), "Finance Department, European Theater of Operations," January, 1946, Office Chief of Finance.

Conner, R. B., Col. "Currency Control, European Theater," FIND 123 (Europe), June 19, 1947, Office Chief of Finance.

"Currency Control," in Occupation Forces in Europe Series, 1945–46, Office Chief of Military History.

Feyereisen, Paul A., Lt. Col. "Foreign Currency Balances of the United States Army After World War II—Their Utilization," September 7, 1949, Plans and Policy Office, Office of Army Comptroller, World War II Records Division.

"First Year of the Occupation, The," in Occupation Forces in Europe Series, 1945–46, Office Chief of Military History.

"History of Base Section Two, Services of Supply, India-Burma Theater," May 21, 1945 to December 31, 1945, Office Chief of Military History.

"History of Central Pacific Base Command During World War II, Vol. V, Historical Review Covering Activities of Construction Service," September 15, 1945, Office Chief of Military History.

"History of Fiscal and Finance Activities in the Middle Pacific from December 7, 1941 to September 2, 1945," Office Chief of Military History.

"History of Fiscal and Finance Operations, Services of Supply, China–Burma–India Theater, from Activation Through December 31, 1944," January 15, 1945, Federal Records Center.

"History of Fiscal Services, 1940–1945," Office Chief of Military History.

"History of the Fiscal Section," Headquarters, Advance Section, Communications Zone, Office of the Finance Officer, APO 11, U.S. Army, Federal Records Center.

"History of the Services of Supply, China–Burma–India, Appendix 13, Fiscal and Finance Operations, February 28, 1942 to October 24, 1944," Office Chief of Military History.

Koch, Ralph A., Col., Lt. Col. Harold W. Uhrbrock, and Lt. Col. Maynard N. Levenick. "The Activities of the Finance Department in the European Theater of Operations," Study 75, Report of the General Board, United States Forces, European theater, File R 013/1, 1946, Federal Records Center.

Ruth, Harold S., Col. "Currency Control, United States Army Forces, Pacific, 1945–1946," October 2, 1951, Office Chief of Finance.

PERSONAL INTERVIEWS

Archer, T. W., Lt. Col., February 3, 1954.
Ashworth, T. D., Col., July 26, 1955.
Benton, D. E., Maj., December 21, 1956.
Clos, Delavan C., Lt. Col., February 15, 1954.
Coakley, Robert W., Dr., March 31, 1954.
Feyereisen, Paul A., Col., August 24, 1955.
Graham, Raymond E., Lt. Col., February 3, 1954.
Gretser, George R., Col., March 30, 1954.
Jenks, Royal G., Col. (Ret.), August 17, 1955.
"Joe," April 27, 1954.
Koch, Ralph A., Col., July 12, 1954.
Miller, A. H., Col., August 15, 1956.
Osborn, Gordon D., June 24, 1955.
Routh, Ross H., Col., June 24, 1954.
Tullington, B. J., Col., August 2, 1955.
Whitney, Lester A., April 5, 1963.

GOVERNMENT DOCUMENTS

Occupation Currency Transactions, Hearings Before the Committees on Appropriations, Armed Services, and Banking and Currency, United States Senate, 80th Congress, 1st Session (Washington: Government Printing Office, 1947).

The Parliamentary Debates. 5th Series. Vol. 433. London: Her Majesty's Stationery Office, February 18, 1947. Frequently referred to as *Hansard.*

Report on House Resolution 150, Appendix A, signed Henry L. Stimson, Secretary of War, April 28, 1945. (Washington: Government Printing Office, 1945).

Sixth Annual Report of the United States High Commissioner to the Philippine Islands to the President and Congress of the United States Covering the Fiscal Year July 1, 1941, to June 30, 1942 (Washington: Government Printing Office, 1942).

U.S. Congress, House of Representatives, *Military Payment Certificates,* Hearings Before a Subcommittee of the Committee on House Administration, 84th Congress, 2nd Session (Washington: Government Printing Office, 1956).

U.S. Treasury Department and War Department, *Joint Statement . . . [on] Allied Military Currency,* Treasury release, August 2, 1943, Press Service No. 37–85. (Washington: Government Printing Office, 1943).

GENERAL AND SPECIFIC HISTORIES

Bank for International Settlements. *Italy's Economic and Financial Position in the Summer of 1947.* Basle, 1947.

Banque de France. *Compte Rendu des Opérations.* Paris: Imprimeries Paul Dupont, 1947.

Block, Henry Simon, and Bert F. Hoselitz. *Economies of Military Occupation.* Rev. ed. Chicago: University of Chicago Press, 1944.

Chambers, Whittaker. *Witness.* New York: Random House, 1952.

Chang, Kia-Ngau. *The Inflationary Spiral, The Experience in China, 1939–1950.* Cambridge: The Technology Press of Massachusetts Institute of Technology, and New York: John Wiley and Sons, Inc., 1958.

Dulles, Eleanor Lansing. *The French Franc, 1914–1928, The Facts and Their Interpretation.* New York: The Macmillan Company, 1929.

Edgeworth, F. Y. *Currency and Finance in Time of War.* London: Oxford University Press, 1918.

――――. *On the Relations of Political Economy to War.* London: Oxford University Press, n.d.

Ellis, Howard S. *Exchange Control in Central Europe.* Cambridge: Harvard University Press, 1941.

Feilchenfeld, Ernst H. *The International Economic Law of Belligerent*

Occupation. Washington: Carnegie Endowment for International Peace, 1942.

Hunt, I. L., Col. *American Military Government of Occupied Germany, 1919–1920, Report of the Officer in Charge of Civil Affairs, Third Army and American Forces in Germany*, n.p., 1920.

Kasten, Helmut. *Währung und Reichskreditkassen in den Besetzten Gebieten.* Berlin: Bank-Verlag, 1941.

Lagrenée, Jacques. *Le Problème Monétaire en France après les Guerres de 1870–1871 et 1914–1918.* Paris: Les Presses Universitaires de France, 1923.

Lester, Richard A. "International Aspects of Wartime Monetary Experience," in *Essays in International Finance* (Princeton, 1944).

Logistical History of NATOUSA-MTOUSA. Naples: G. Montanino, 1945.

Loria, Achille. *Le Peripezie Monetarie Della Guerra.* Milano: Fratelli Treves, Editori, 1920.

Millett, John D. *The Organization and Role of the Army Service Forces.* Washington: Office of the Chief of Military History, 1954.

Niebuhr, Reinhold. *The Irony of American History.* New York: Charles Scribner's Sons, 1952.

Ouchi, Hyoye. *Financial and Monetary Situation in Post-War Japan.* New York: Institute of Pacific Relations, 1947.

Popovics, Alexander. *Das Geldwesen im Kriege.* Wien: Holder-Pilcher-Tempsky, 1925.

Risch, Erna. *Quartermaster Support of the Army, A History of the Corps, 1775–1939.* Washington: Office of the Quartermaster General, 1962.

Rogers, James Harvey. *The Process of Inflation in France, 1914–1927.* New York: Columbia University Press, 1929.

Romanus, Charles F., and Riley Sunderland. *Stilwell's Command Problems.* Washington: Office of the Chief of Military History, 1955.

Sherwin, Stephen F. *Monetary Policy in Continental Western Europe, 1944–1952.* ("Wisconsin Commerce Studies," Vol. II, No. 2.) Madison, 1956.

Southard, Frank A., Jr. *The Finances of European Liberation.* New York: King's Crown Press, 1946.

Spahr, Walter E. *Allied Military Currency.* New York: The Economists' National Committee on Monetary Policy, 1943.

Stamp, Sir Josiah C. *The Financial Aftermath of War.* London: Ernest Benn Ltd., 1932.

PERIODICALS

Abbott, Alfred A., Maj. "The Army as a Banker," *Army Information Digest* (August, 1947).

Bennett, Jack. "The German Currency Reform," *The Annals of the American Academy of Political and Social Science,* CCLXVII (1950).

Bratter, Herbert. "Invasion Currency," *Banking,* XXXVI (1943).

"Fixing the Lira Rate," *The Economist* (London) CXLV (1943).

Klopstock, Fred H. "Monetary Reform in Western Germany," *Journal of Political Economy,* LVII (1949).

Mendershausen, Horst. "Prices, Money and the Distribution of Goods in Postwar Germany," *American Economic Review,* XXXIX (1949).

Mundt, Karl E. "How Harry Dexter White Pulled Wires for Russia," *U. S. News and World Report* (December 25, 1953).

"One Man's Greed," *Time,* LXII (November 23, 1953).

Rundell, Walter, Jr. "Invasion Currency: A U.S. Army Fiscal Problem in World War II," *The Southwestern Social Science Quarterly,* XLIII (1962).

————. "Paying the POW in World War II," *Military Affairs,* XXII (1958).

Southard, Frank A., Jr. "Some European Currency and Exchange Experiences: 1943–1946," *Essays in International Finance* (Princeton, 1946).

Stokes, Richard L. "The Astounding Soviet Swindle of American Taxpayers," *The Reader's Digest,* LXII (1953).

Tamagna, Frank M. "The Fixing of Foreign Exchange Rates," *Journal of Political Economy,* LII (1945).

NEWSPAPERS

Manchester *Guardian*
New York *Herald-Tribune*
New York *Times*
Stars and Stripes (London)

Air Corps, U.S. Army, records of,
Allied Forces Headquarters, 25
Allied military marks: European use
   of theater's, 30, 34; Russian distribution of, 33, 36, 41–44 *passim;*
   four occupying powers use of, 40,
   41, 42; Treasury's design of, 42;
   Elizabeth Bentley's testimony on,
   43; Russian-printed, 44, 45, 46,
   87; overdraft in, 45; American-
   printed, 45, 46; mentioned, 32, 33,
   35, 41, 45, 46, 87, 91
American forces in Germany, World
   War I, 60
Appropriation, Congressional, 3, 4,
   82, 89, 90
Archer, Capt. T. W., 26–27
Army post offices: in North Africa,
   25; in European theater, 29, 53;
   in Far East, 66; in Berlin, 71, 76,
   77; in Frankfurt, 76; as collection
   agency, 81; closed in Pacific command, 86; opened in Pacific command, 87; mentioned, 55
Army Service Forces, 5, 31, 35, 53
Australia, economy of, 6, 10–11

Austria, scrip introduced in, 87;
   mentioned, 84
Axis agents, using dollars, 21, 23
Axis powers, use of dollars, 6, 7

Balkans, currency used in, 55–56, 68
Bank of Chosen, notes of, 85
Bank of Japan, 82
Banque de France, francs of, 29
Barclay's Bank, in Egypt, 22
Belgium, scrip introduced in, 87
Bentley, Elizabeth, 43
Berlin district: Russian-printed marks
   in, 46; transmission of funds from,
   48, 75; pay disbursements in, 71;
   deficit in, 72; use of chit books
   in, 77
Berlin, Germany: black market, 46–
   49, 70; transmission of funds from,
   74
Bernstein, Col. Bernard, 36–37, 53
Black market: source of overdraft,
   4; in China, 16–19; in United
   Kingdom, 20; prices in Germany,
   50; control of, 52; in Italy, 54–55;
   in France, 56–58; in Japan, 63–65,

117

66, 73; scrip in, 81; conversion of profits of, 86
British Army: scrip, 84; overdraft, 89
British War Office, 90
Brooklyn, N.Y., 55
Budget division, War Department: on gambling profits, 37; on currency control books, 69; at conference on scrip, 84
Budget officer, War Department, 84, 85
Bureau of Engraving and Printing: supplies francs, 28; and mark printing plates, 43; designs scrip, 86–87; mentioned, 42
Burmese military rupees, 82

Cairo, Egypt, 22
Cairo Military District, dollar purchase of, 21
Camp Lucky Strike, 47
Camp Miles Standish, Mass., 47
Canteen goods, on black market, 89
Canteen money (British scrip), 84
Carter, Maj. Gen. Arthur H.: as fiscal director, 5; response to Treasury, 31–32
Casablanca, Algeria, yellow seal dollars in, 23
Casablanca conference, 25, 57
Central Pacific command, use of Hawaiian overstamp dollars in, 15
Central Reserve Bank (Chinese), notes of, 17, 66
Certification of funds: in European theater, 37, 52, 74; in Japan, 63, 69
Chambers, Whittaker, 42–43
Chief of staff, European theater, 70
Chiefs of Staff, Combined, 42
China Clearing Board, 19–20
China, economy of, 8
China theater: savings program, 12; currency control in, 66; civilians returning from, 67; mentioned, 95 n.20

China–Burma–India theater: savings program, 12; split, 95 n.20
Chinese government, expenditures for U.S. Army, 67
Chinese national currency, 17–18, 66–67
Chit books, in Berlin district, 77
Chungking, China, gold prices in, 66
Churchill, Prime Minister Winston S., 20; at Casablanca conference, 25, 57
Circular 50, pp. 77, 78
Circular 52, p. 85
Circular 82, pp. 77, 78, 79
Circular 139, pp. 70, 72, 75, 77, 78
Civil affairs division, War Department on gambling profits, 36–37; on scrip, 84
Civilian employees, War Department, 86, 89
Clos, Maj. Delavan C., 74
Cobbs, Brig. Gen. Nicholas H.: on German currency, 32, 33–35; at lower echelon, 38–39; mentioned, 78
Coins, disappearance of, in North Africa, 25
Commodities: in Germany, 44; in France, 57–58; in Japan, 65; in China, 66
Communications zone, European theater, 11, 30, 33, 34, 35, 39, 97 n.39
Communist party, American, 43
Company grade officers, fund transference of, 28–29
Congress, 3, 4, 10, 36, 90
Conversion day: in Japan, 86; in Europe, 87; in Pacific command, 87
Counterfeit currency, 29; measures against, 86–87
Court of St. James, 10
Criminal Investigation Detachment, 49
Currency control: goal of, 3; prewar planning of, 4; uniformity of, 5–6,

7–9; objectives of, 6–7; use of local currencies in, 9; on Pacific islands, 13–16; in China, 16–20; in United Kingdom, 20

Currency control book: in European theater, 53, 71, 72; War Department study of, 69; in Japan, 73; counterfeits of, 73; effect on dependents, 74; Col. Gretser on, 75; Circular 82, effect on, 78; inspections of, 79; mentioned, 76, 78, 83

Currency control card, 51

Currency: invasion type 93 n.*4*; military type, 93 n.*4*

Curtin, John, as Prime Minister of Australia, 11

Cyprus, scrip in, 91

Deficit. *See* overdraft

Denmark, scrip in, 87

Dependency allotments: as savings method, 10; in Australia, 11; in China, 19

Dependents: without currency control books, 74; currency control books of, 77

Disbursing accounts: losses reflected in, 59; in Far East, 65

Disbursing officer. *See* finance officer

Disbursing quartermaster, 60

Discipline: in European theater, 76; problems with scrip, 83

Dollar credits, 3, 10, 38, 40, 55, 57, 63, 65, 66, 75, 81, 85, 86

Dollar: effect on foreign economies, 3, 92; yellow seal type in North Africa, 8–9; in Hawaii, 14; Hawaiian overstamp, 14–15, 83; blue seal type in North Africa, 20; in Egypt, 21; in Naples, 22, 55; in Casablanca, 23; Nazi agents use of, 23; merchant seamen traffic in, 24; in Balkans, 56; reserves, 67; German overstamp, 83; American tourist use of, 91

Dunn, James C., 42

Egypt, dollars in, 21

Egyptian government, 21

Eisenhower, Gen. Dwight D.: as commander, 10; on currency needs, 42; on War Department, 44–45; on currency control, 51, 53; on adjusted franc payment, 58; War Department on, 71–72; mentioned, 76

European theater: German currency in, 32–33; collapse of currency control in, 33–40 *passim;* effect on currency control, 53; on adjusted franc payments, 58; currency control books in, 71; Eisenhower's position on currency control in, 72; 1946 payroll in, 75; Circular 50 in, 77; Circular 82 in, 79; at conference on scrip, 84; conversion to scrip in, 86, 87; mentioned, 28, 29, 30, 51, 52, 54, 61, 68, 69, 73, 76, 78, 85

Exchange: official rate of, 3; in France, 57; in China, 66; fixed rates of, 101 n.*46*; Tamagna on, 102 n.*46*

Federal Reserve Bank (Chinese), notes, 17, 66

Field grade officers, exemptions for, 29, 48

Fifty-sixth finance disbursing section, 75

Finance Department: functions, 4–5; as exchange agency, 22; personnel in Mediterranean theater, 83

Finance officers: responsibilities, 5, 26; on pay restriction, 9; exchanging currency, 17, 62, 85, 86; furnished Chinese currency, 17; in Cairo, 21; confiscate black-market lire, 26; handling counterfeits, 29; instructions to, 33, 34; Russian, 44; on Russian-printed marks, 44–45; of Berlin district, 46; handling net troop pay, 58; on Formosa,

68; on currency control books, 74, 75; on maintenance of currency control, 76

Finance office, U.S. Army, New York, 38

Finance offices: as exchanges in China, 18; as exchanges in Egypt, 21–22; as exchanges in Naples, 22–23; as exchanges in North Africa, 25; as agencies of collection and conversion, 28, 30, 52–53, 57, 71, 81, 86, 106 n.*1*; counterfeits in, 29; at Camp Miles Standish, 47; as exchanges in Japan, 62; of Seventy-eighth division, 75; in Berlin, 71, 76; dependents use of, 77

First Airborne Army, Eleventh Traffic Regulation Group, 74

First Army, 33

First Cavalry Division, 73

Fiscal director, Army Service Forces, 21. *See also* Carter, Maj. Gen. Arthur H.

Fiscal director, European theater: on scrip, 30; in subordinate headquarters, 39; on currency controls, 53; on currency control books, 70, 73; mentioned, 59, 83. *See also* Cobbs, Brig. Gen. Nicholas H., and Koch, Col. Ralph A.

Flowers, wired from Germany, 48–49

Formosa, dollars used on, 68

Franc (Belgian), overdraft in, 88

Franc devaluation: in 1945, p. 58; in 1919, p. 60

Franc: in French provisional government, 20; exchange rate of, 57

Franc payments, adjustment of, 58

France, scrip in, 87

Frankfurt, Germany, 50, 76

French Committee of National Liberation, 25, 28

French provisional government: in North Africa, 8–9; at Casablanca conference, 57

Funding: on Okinawa, 16; on Formosa, 68

G-1, European theater: on German currencies, 34; currency control responsibility, 39, 51, 54; funds transmission, 52–53; on currency control books, 70, 73, 76; on Circular 139, p. 77; on scrip, 78, 83

G-1, War Department: on converting gambling profits, 37; at conference on scrip, 84

G-5, Supreme Headquarters, Allied Expeditionary Forces, 33–34, 36, 53

Gambling profits: convertibility of, 37–38; in Berlin district, 48, 71

Geneva convention, of 1929 (POW), 89

German government, on currency control, 82

Germany: occupation economy of, 41, 49–51; scrip introduced in, 87

Gold prices, in China, 66

Governments, in exile, 27

Great Britain, scrip in, 87. *See also* United Kingdom

Gresham's law, 23

Gretser, Col. George R., 46, 74–75

Guadalcanal, 15

Guilders, overdraft in, 88

Hall, A. W., 42

Haskins and Sells, 5

Hawaii, Territory of, 6, 14

Heliopolis, Egypt, 22

Hilldring, Maj. Gen. John J., 36

Hiroshima, Japan, 91

Hitler, Adolf, 50

Hokkaido, 62

Holland, scrip in, 87

Honshu, 62

India, 6

India–Burma theater: on scrip, 83; mentioned, 95 n.*20*

Indo-China, currency speculation in, 18
Inflation: in Germany, 50; in France, 56; in Japan, 63; in China, 66
Insurance programs, 10
Italian government, 27
Italy: economy of, 54; currency shortage in, 62; scrip in, 87

Japan: economy of, 63; scrip in, 87; mentioned, 91
Japanese Army, 8, 15, 18; scrip in, 82
Japanese government, services from, 88
Judge advocate general, on withholding pay, 10

Koch, Col. Ralph A., 77, 83
Korea: scrip in, 87; mentioned, 91
Kroner, overdraft in, 88
Kunming, China, 18–19
Kyushu, 62

Leica cameras, 50
Libya, scrip in, 91
Lire, Allied military, 20
London, England, 38
Long position. *See* overdraft
Loughry, Maj. Gen. Howard K., 4–5
Luxembourg, scrip in, 87

MacArthur, Gen. Douglas: as commander, 11; on type A yen, 85
McNarney, Gen. Joseph T.: on discipline in European theater, 76; on scrip, 78
Mackay Radio Corporation, flowers cabled by, 48
Manchester *Guardian,* on troop spending, 10
Marks, overdraft in, 88
Marshall, Gen. George C., 42
Mediterranean area, 20, 22, 24, 25
Mediterranean Base Section, 23
Mediterranean theater: formula for currency control, 26–27; in postwar period, 55; adopts currency control books, 75; opposes scrip, 83; at conference on scrip, 84; conversion to scrip, 86; mentioned, 85, 94 n.*17*
Merchant seamen, as speculators, 24
Middle East command, on scrip, 83
Middle Pacific command, use of Hawaiian overstamp dollar by, 15
Milan, Italy, 26
Military Government Law No. 51, contravened, 33–35
Military payment certificates: proposed, 84; plans for, 85; approved, 86; series, 461 issued, 87. *See also* Scrip
Military payment order: payment in, suggested by Treasury, 80; *Verrechnungsscheine* similar to, 82; defined, 106 n.*1*
Missionaries, in China, 19
Morale: in China, 18; in European theater, 39, 52, 76; implications with scrip, 83
Morgenthau, Henry, Jr., 42, 43

Naples, Italy, 22, 25
National Bank of Egypt, 21
National City Bank, New York, 19
Navy, use of dollars in Hawaii by, 14
Navy Department, on dissipation of overdraft, 88–89
Nazi agents, 23
Net troop pay, 56, 57, 58, 100 n.*27*
Netherlands East Indies, military guilders in, 82
New York *Herald-Tribune,* 71, 84
New York *Times,* 64, 71, 76, 85
New Zealand, economy of, 8
Ninth Army, 33, 54
"No rate" funds, 18
Non-fraternization, in Germany, 33, 45
Normandy invasion, 27, 28

North Africa: invasion of, 8–9; currency shortage in, 62; scrip in, 87
North African theater, circular on currencies in, 33

Occupation costs, transfer of, 52
Office of the Chief of Finance: responsibilities of, 4, 5; at conference on scrip, 84
Office of the Fiscal Director, Army Service Forces: organization of, 5; on prohibition of German currency, 35; on conversion of gambling profits, 37; request for report on marks, 44–45; designs currency control book, 53, 69–70
Okinawa: campaign of, 16; type B yen on, 62; and scrip, 87
Operations division, War Department, at conference on scrip, 84
Oran, Algeria, 23
Overdraft: in Treasury, 7, 88; in Allied military marks, 45; in Germany, 48; in Pacific command, 65; in Berlin district, 72; dissipation of, 88; British, 89–90; mentioned, 71, 81, 86, 89, 90, 92

Pacific command U.S. Army Forces in the Pacific: occupation of Japan, 61–62; War Department on, 63; failure of currency control in, 66, 68; at conference on scrip, 84; scrip in, 86, 87; dissipation of overdraft in, 88; mentioned, 64, 69, 83, 84–85
Paris, France, currency control in, 47, 59
Parliament, consideration of overdraft by, 89–90
Patterson, Robert P.: on franc exchange rate, 57; on scrip, 85
Patton, Gen. George S., 37
Pay: exchange of, 3; restriction of, 9–10, 94 n.*17*; inviolability of, 36
Pershing, Gen. John J., 28

Persian Gulf command, 24
Personal transfer accounts: 3; in Southwest Pacific Area, 11; in Italy, 26; in European theater, 28; New York Finance Office, U.S. Army, handling of, 38; in Japan, 62; in Far East, 65; definition of, 93 n.*2*
Personnel officer, certification of funds by, 28–29, 74
Pesos (Philippine): military type, 82; overdraft in, 88
Pforzheimer, Col. Carl H., Jr.: on currency control, 47–48, 107 n.*16*; on franc exchange rate, 57; on currency control books, 69–70; as chairman of conference on scrip, 84; mentioned, 51
Post exchanges: soldier spending in, 11; goods from, 28, 49; in Italy, 55; in Far East, 65, 66, 73; in Berlin, 71, 76, 77; as collection agency, 81; in Pacific command, 86; in Pacific command, 87; purchases from overdraft for, 89; mentioned, 77
Post Office Department, U.S. investigation of money orders, 55
Postal money order: as method of establishing dollar credits, 3; in Southwest Pacific Area, 11; in China, 19; in European theater, 28, 75; investigations of, 32; in Italy, 55; in Japan, 62; mentioned, 30
Pounds, United Kingdom, overdraft in, 88
Price index: in Germany, 50; in France, 56–57; in Japan, 63
Prisoner of war accounts, 89, 109 n. 34
Property accountability, in Japan, 65
Provost marshal, 22, 26, 55
Public opinion, on currency control, 51, 90

Pumpkin papers. *See* Chambers, Whittaker

Quadripartite policy, in Germany, 39–40, 41–42
Quartermaster Corps, 102 n.*56*
Quartermaster sales stores: in Japan, 65, 66, 73; in Berlin, 71, 76, 77; in Pacific command, 86, 87
Quasi-official funds, 59

Red Army: Allied military marks, disbursement of by, 41; finance officers, 44
Reichskreditkassenscheine, similarity to scrip, 46, 82, 84, 91
Reichsmarks: for exchange, 29–30; handling of, 32–36; prohibition of, 37
Rental collections, applied against overdraft, 89
Rentenmarks: presented for exchange, 30; instructions for handling, 32–33
Reparation claim, overdraft as, 72
Rials, overdraft in, 88
Richards, Maj. Gen. George J.: as War Department budget officer, 35; on currency control books, 69; on yen experiment, 86
Roer River, crossing, 33
Rome, Italy, 26
Roosevelt, Franklin D.: on troop spending, 10; at Casablanca conference, 25, 57; on troop pay in World War I, 28
Rothnie, Col. K. B., 64
Rumania, currency in, 56
Rupees, overdraft in, 88
Ruth, Col. Harold S., 65, 66, 83, 85
Ryukyus Islands. *See* Okinawa

Savings program: aim of, 10; in European theater, 11; in Mediterranean theater, 11–12; in Australia, 12; in China–Burma–India theater, 12; in China theater, 12, 67; on Okinawa, 16; mentioned, 31, 94 n. 17
Schillings, overdraft in, 88
Scrip: Eureopean theater and the fiscal director, 39; European theater G-1 on, 78; Gen. McNarney on, 79; features of, 81, 83; Mediterranean theater on, 83; Middle East command on, 83; civil affairs division of War Department on, 84; Pacific command trial of, 85; conversion to, 86; introduction of, 87, 104 n.2; collections, applied against overdraft, 90; retention of, 91; withdrawal of, 91; mentioned, 84
Second Armored Division, 46
Secret Service, U.S., 29
Secretary of War: letter from Vinson, 80; proposal for scrip, 84; on scrip, 85, 86; on dissipation of overdraft, 89. *See also* Patterson, Robert P.
Secretary of the Treasury: handles adjusted franc payments, 58; informed of yen experiment, 85. *See also* Morgenthau, Henry, Jr., and Vinson, Fred M.
Senate Committees of Appropriations, Banking and Currency, Armed Services, hearings on occupation currency transactions, 89
Services of Supply, European theater, 39
Seventh Air Force, use of dollars in Hawaii by, 14
Seventh Army, 33, 46
Seventy-eighth division, finance office, 75
Shanghai, China, gold prices in, 66
Shikoku, 62
Sixth Corps, finance office, 59
Smith, Lt. Gen. Walter Bedell, 34, 51

Soldiers' deposits: type of saving, 3; in Southwest Pacific Area, 11; in China–Burma–India theater, 12; black-market profits converted to, 47; in Japan, 62; in Far East, 65; definition of, 93n.2; mentioned, 30

South Pacific Area, 15

South Pacific, military operations in, 8

Southwest Pacific Area, restriction of troop pay in, 10–11. *See also* Australia

Speculation: with dollars and piastres, 18–19; in Egypt, 21–22; by Arab shoeshine boys, 23; Lester on, 101–102n.*46*

Stars and Stripes, 27, 71

State, Department of: negotiations with Egyptian government, 21; on currency printing plates, 42; mentioned, 18, 57

Supreme Headquarters, Allied Expeditionary Forces (SHAEF), 33–36 *passim*, 38, 44

Switzerland, scrip introduced in, 87

Taylor, William H., 32

Tenth Army, restriction of pay by, 16

Theater Service Forces, European Theater, 39

Third Army, 33

Third Reich: fall of, 50; transfer of occupation costs, 100n.*27*

Time, 42

Tokyo, Japan, 83

Tonga, economy of, 15–16

Travelers' checks, 87

Treasury Department: on currency control, 9; on speculation in China, 19; negotiations with Egyptian government, 21; queries War Department, 31; and currency printing plates, 42; and France, 59; checks, 66, 106n.*1*; China's credit in, 67; on scrip, 80; on breakdown of currency control, 80–81; on dissipation of overdraft, 88–89; mentioned, 7, 8, 18, 25, 32, 37, 43, 44, 52, 57, 67, 72, 83, 84, 90, 91

Trieste, scrip introduced in, 87

Tripoli, Libya, 22

Truman, Harry S.: on adjusted franc payment, 58; on dissipation of overdraft, 89

Tullington, Col. B. J., 15

Twelfth Army Group, 33, 54

Twenty-second Corps, 46, 74

United Kingdom: troop spending in, 10; currency control in, 20

U.S.S.R., transfer of occupation costs, 100n.*27*

U.S. Army Forces in the Middle East, 21

U.S. Army Forces in the Pacific. *See* Pacific command

U.S. Army Forces, Pacific Ocean Areas, 16

V-E Day, 30, 55

V-J Day, 62, 66, 67

Vatican City, 55

Verrechnungsscheine, 82

Vienna, Austria, 76

Vinson, Fred M., 80

War bonds: as a means of saving, 3; in Southwest Pacific Area, 11; in China–Burma–India theater, 12; in European theater, 28; in Far East, 65; mentioned, 30

War Department: and currency control action, 4, 53; on currency control, 9, 104n.*16*; on adjusted franc payment, 58; on Pacific command, 63; on currency control books, 70; on European theater, 71–72; interest in scrip, 77, 78;

and the Treasury, 81; queries theaters on scrip, 83; communiqués on scrip, 84; conference on scrip, 84; dissipating overdraft, 88–89; on liquidation of overdraft, 90; mentioned, 5, 8, 10, 11, 12, 13, 18, 31, 32, 35–38 *passim*, 43, 44, 47, 51, 52, 57, 66, 69, 75, 78, 79, 80, 83, 85
War Shipping Administration, 24
Washington, D.C., 44, 72
Washington National Airport, 43
Wehrmacht, currency of, 46, 82

West African district, European theater, 87
Western Union, 77
White, Harry Dexter, 42–43
White House, press conference, 28
Winant, John G., 10
World War I, currency experience, 28, 59

Yen: Imperial, 62, 63, 85, 86, 91; type B, 62, 63, 85, 86; type A, 69, 85, 86, 87, 104 n.*1*; scrip, 82; bloc, 83; experiment in Pacific command, 85–86; overdraft in, 88